RISK IT ALL

ISBN (Paperback): 979-8-9926076-0-4
ISBN (E-Book): 979-8-9926076-1-1

For permissions, inquiries, or any other requests, please contact City Line Press at support@citylinepress.com. AMDG.

RISK IT ALL

The Epic Battle of 25 Maverick Traders and the Chicago Mercantile Exchange

Rick Kessler
&
Michael Alan

CONTENTS

CHAPTER ONE

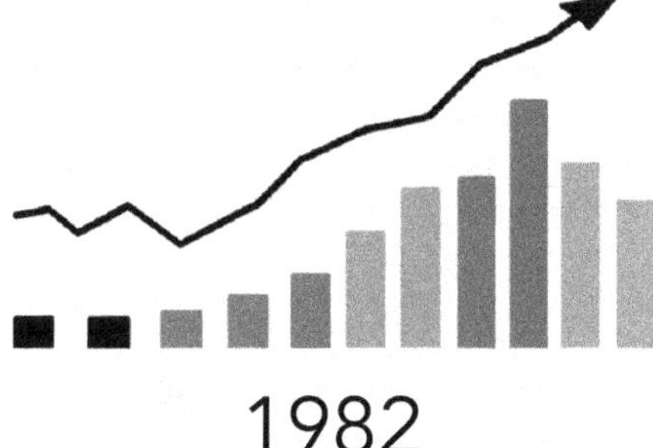

1982

I clutched the metal pole tighter and tried to ground myself as the train hurtled through Chicago's maze of tracks. My reflection in the grimy window stared back at me, pale and determined. With every passing minute, the weight of what awaited me sank deeper into my bones. Today was my first day at the Chicago Mercantile Exchange (CME), and while I had dreamed of this moment, now it was all too real.

You've worked for this. You've earned it.

I repeated the words silently, like a mantra, trying to steady the flutter in my chest. I thought back to those long nights spent hunched over textbooks, learning the intricacies of futures markets, financial modeling, and risk management. I had memorized charts until my eyes blurred and studied market movements with the intensity of someone desperate to find patterns in chaos.

Supply and demand curves, technical analysis, trading strategies... I'd made it my mission to know them all. Nothing had come easily; every step had been earned through grit and determination.

I recalled my mentor's words from a year ago: *"Knowledge can make you a trader, but instinct makes you independent."* It had become my guiding star, pushing me beyond memorizing theory and into the complex dance of practical experience. I had watched the markets for months on end, testing myself with simulated trades, tracking trends, and learning to anticipate how even the slightest change in international policy could ripple across the commodities floor. Becoming an independent trader was my goal—no, my obsession—but I knew I'd have to start at the bottom.

I'll get there, I told myself, even as doubt threatened to creep in. I wanted the freedom to call my own shots, to be my own master in a world that rewarded boldness and risk-taking. But first, I had to survive today.

This is step one.

To distract myself from the nerves that clawed at my insides, I unfolded the crumpled newspaper tucked under my arm. The headline jumped out at me in bold print: *"The Chicago Mercantile Exchange: A High-Stakes World Where Seconds Define Fortunes."* I smoothed the page with trembling hands and began to read.

> In the heart of Chicago's financial district, the Chicago Mercantile Exchange stands as a bastion of economic power and frenzied energy. Here, men and women battle with words, gestures, and quick calculations that decide the fate of millions of dollars each day. The trading pits are renowned for their intensity—where fortunes are made and lost in the blink of an eye.
>
> "It's not just numbers, it's combat," said veteran trader Howard Ames. "You come here prepared to win, or you don't come at all."

> Founded in the late 19th century, the Exchange has evolved into a modern-day coliseum of commerce, handling everything from agricultural commodities to futures contracts. For many, this is not just a job but a calling, an adrenaline-charged theater of ambition, grit, and unrelenting pressure. But beyond the spectacle lies a scandal—whispers of manipulation, insider deals, and backroom negotiations that may be casting a complex web around this institution.
>
> "You have to keep your eyes wide open," one anonymous broker said. "One misstep, and you're out."

I stopped reading and stared blankly at the page. *One misstep, and you're out.* The words echoed in my mind. I wasn't naïve; I knew the stakes were high but reading it here in black and white made the entire situation feel like I was on the edge of a cliff, about to leap into unknown waters. A brusque voice interrupted my thoughts.

"Mind if I sit here son?" An elderly man in a rumpled suit gestured at the seat beside me. I nodded absently, folding the paper and clutching it to my chest as if it might shield me from the reality hurtling closer with each station stop. The Exchange was where dreams were forged or shattered. I wanted to believe I was ready, but my pulse hammered a nervous rhythm, betraying my doubts.

The old man peered at the article that shook violently on my bouncing knee. "First day in the working world?" he asked, a knowing smile playing at his lips.

"Yes," I replied, trying to force some levity into my voice, "independent trading." He gave a nod of approval.

"Been there myself," he said, his tone softer now. "Good luck, son. You'll need it."

"Thank you," I smiled kindly at him before picking up the paper and pretending to read for the rest of the train ride.

This is it.

I'd been waiting for this day since I first heard the words "Chicago Mercantile Exchange" whispered amongst the hopeful and ambitious in my neighborhood. The words conjured images of wealth, prestige, and the pulse of a city's economic heart, and today I was stepping into that very world. The train lurched, snapping me out of my reverie.

I adjusted my tie, feeling its constriction at my throat, and tugged nervously on the sleeves of my oversized suit jacket. I wanted to look the part, to be the man who walked confidently onto the trading floor and held his own. My family's sacrifices that put me through college had all led to this moment. I thought of my father's calloused hands, of my mother's quiet prayers whispered over the dinner table.

They believed in me, and today I had to believe in myself.

As the train pulled into the station, I said goodbye to the elderly man and stepped out into the sea of commuters, my steps quickened with each breath. The wind howled between the towering buildings, a cruel reminder of how small I felt in this vast city. I forced myself to push onward, weaving through the crowd and streets until the steel-and-glass behemoth of the Mercantile Exchange loomed before me.

Inside, the building seemed to hum with energy—as if it could sense the ambitions of everyone who entered. The air was thick with the tang of sweat and adrenaline. The weight of fortunes rising and falling hung in the air. I passed through security and rode the elevator up to the floor, feeling each second stretch.

I wiped my damp palms on my pants and whispered to myself, "You can do this, Michael."

When the elevator doors slid open, it felt like stepping into another universe. The cacophony hit me first; a roar of voices, each trying to outshout the other. It was a chaotic symphony of ambition. My eyes darted from the brokers in neon jackets gesticulating wildly to the price boards flashing numbers. The floor itself was a mass of humanity. For a moment, I could only stand there, bewildered and overdressed.

“Buy three contracts at seventy-four!” one broker shouted; his face flushed.

“Sell five contracts at seventy-four and a quarter!” came the immediate response from across the pit.

“Who’s taking seventy-four and a half?” a third trader bellowed, waving a stack of paper in the air.

“Got it here! Seventy-four and a half!” yelled a fourth voice, his hand shot up to seal the deal. Palms slapped together, a physical contract in this verbal warzone.

“Rookies need to stick to the edges if they want to live.” An attractive woman with distracting red lips breezed past me. Her hands moved with swift elegance to signal a bid, the motion practiced and precise. I watched, mesmerized, as her piercing eyes settled back on me, a hint of challenge glimmering there.

“Unless you’re here to decorate the floor, pretty boy.”

I’d heard stories about women like her, the sirens of the trading floor. She looked at me like she’d eat me alive, which part of me found thrilling, but I knew better than to let my guard down.

“Maybe I’m here to rearrange the décor,” I replied smoothly. “You know, shake things up a bit.” A smirk tugged at the corners of her painted lips.

“Is that so?” she said, stepping closer. “I like a man who isn’t afraid to say what’s on his mind.” Her gaze traveled over me appraisingly. “Don’t shake things up too much around here, I would hate to see that pretty face crushed.”

“I’ll keep that in mind,” I returned calmly, refusing to look away. If she wanted to test me, I wasn’t about to break. “But I’m not here to be careful.”

“Interesting.” She lingered for a beat. “I’ll be watching you, handsome.” She winked seductively and turned back to the fray, her presence like a storm passing through.

“Michael!” A familiar voice cut through my thoughts. I turned to see Dave Patterson swaggering toward me, his grin as wide and confident as ever. He looked exactly as I remembered him: brash, flamboyant, and the embodiment of everything I wanted to become.

"Stay clear of that vixen, trust me." He said in his thick Irish accent and blew her a kiss which she dismissed with a sharp roll of her eyes. "So, kid, what do you think so far?" Dave gestured toward the chaos of the floor.

"It's not at all what I expected." I looked around in admiration.

"You're in for a hell of a ride!" He clapped me on the back. "So, what'd you study to get yourself thrown to the wolves here?"

"Economics and finance," I replied. "I read everything I could on futures trading, poured over charts, market trends, you name it." I paused, resisting the urge to say more.

Don't sound desperate to impress.

Dave raised an eyebrow. "Textbooks and theories, huh? Bet you got the top marks, too."

"I did what I had to do," I said, bracing myself for the inevitable jab.

"Books are fine for fancy talk," he said with a dismissive wave of his hand, "but this?" He gestured around the trading floor. "This place will teach you more in a week than any class ever could. Ever placed a bet with your rent money, kid?"

"No," I admitted, feeling a twinge of defensiveness.

"Good," he said, surprising me. "Means you've got something left to lose. Just make sure you keep it." He flashed a grin before his expression grew serious. "But remember, nothing beats experience. So, stay sharp and don't get distracted." The weight of his words pressed on me. Dave led me deeper into the chaos, pointing out key figures as we passed.

"See that guy over there?" he said, gesturing toward a man with a booming laugh and a fistful of tickets. "Will Lawrence. Legendary power broker. You'll learn quick that his vices are everyone's business, but no one dares cross him."

I tried to absorb it all as the information came faster. Dave's voice was a lifeline in the storm, and I clung to every word. We reached the S&P 500 futures pit, a circular arena where brokers jostled and yelled, their faces red with exertion. This was where I'd be working, and the thought made my heart pound.

"Owen!" My friend's name made me turn expectantly to see him towering over the crowd, his blue jacket stark against the bright colors.

"He'll show you the ropes," Dave said with finality as he disappeared into the crowd and shouted obscenities.

"Michael, my man! Don't look so spooked, you'll get the hang of it," Owen said reassuringly. "It's like swimming—you'll eventually learn to keep your head above water. We'll start you off with the basics, follow me."

The rest of the day became a blur of activities as I shadowed Owen. I watched him deftly handle his trades, his movements precise and confident. He explained the rhythms of the pit, the subtle signals traders used, and the unspoken rules that governed every interaction.

"It's all about reading people," he said as his eyes scanned the crowd. "You have to know when someone's bluffing and when they're serious. And trust me, there's a lot of bluffing." I frantically committed every word to memory but stopped when a sudden shout drew my attention. Two brokers were nose-to-nose, veins bulging as they hurled insults at each other across the floor.

"That's my trade, you son of a—"

"Like hell it is!"

Their fists clenched and for a moment it looked like it might come to blows. The surrounding traders kept at their work, their eyes flickering toward the drama before quickly darting away like spectators at a prizefight who'd seen it all before.

I turned to Owen, who was chuckling at the ordeal. "Are they serious?"

"Don't worry Mike, it happens all the time," he said casually. "High stakes, high tempers. Nobody wants to lose face out here. But they'll cool off." Sure enough, the altercation ended as quickly as it began, and both men returned to their trades as if nothing had happened.

"That's... normal?" I asked, still incredulous.

"Welcome to the floor," Owen said with a smirk. "Everyone here is one bad bet away from losing their minds. And don't forget, that means you too." Despite the frenetic pace, I felt a thrill each time a trade was completed.

This was power. Raw, unfiltered, and intoxicating power.

I was in awe but as the hours wore on, the high was fleeting and I noticed things that unsettled me. Cracks began to show. A whispered conversation caught my attention, but I brushed it off along with the rest of the babble. I watched curiously as brokers slipped away for hushed meetings. Owen caught me staring at one such exchange and pulled me aside.

"Listen, Michael, whatever you see here or hear, make sure you don't get involved," he warned. "Some things are better left alone. Just do your job and go home. Promise me that?"

"Of course, I promise." It was a rare sight to see Owen McAuliffe lose his composure, but the unease was unmistakable on his face.

I couldn't shake the feeling that something was off. The trading floor was a place of rules and order, but there seemed to be more beneath the surface. A darker hidden world that I was only beginning to glimpse. As the day drew to a close, I found myself alone for a moment, standing at the edge of the pit. I watched as Dave and a group of power brokers gathered, their expressions hard and unreadable. The weight of my ambition weighed down on me and, for the first time, I wondered if I was ready for what lay ahead.

"How's the first day treating you?" Owen's voice pulled me from my thoughts.

"Still trying to wrap my head around it all," I said, glancing around at the whirlwind of activity.

The truth was that the excitement that had filled me earlier was now tinged with a little doubt. I had dreamed of this moment for so long, but I hadn't anticipated the shadows that lurked within the light and the fear of secrecy that came with the job. By the time I left the Exchange that evening, I was buzzing with adrenaline and doubt, my mind swirling with the stark realization that this wasn't just a job; it was a battlefield.

7970
7980

CHAPTER TWO

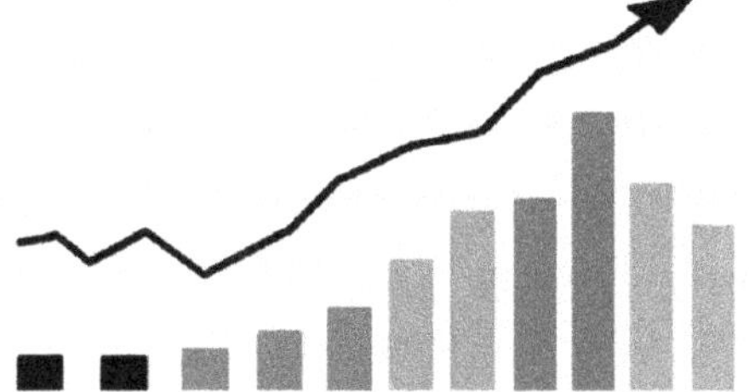

"Listen up, kid. First thing you gotta know—lose the suit. You're gonna wear a yellow jacket from now on. You look like a rookie in that suit. The pit is a madhouse, and you'll stick out like a sore thumb with that getup. Yellow jackets are standard for clerks. You get in, you get out, and you don't make waves. Understand?"

I nodded, glancing around the chaos of the S&P 500 pit. The noise, the constant hand signals, the shouting—there was no way to prepare for it, but I tried to keep my cool.

"Now, you're gonna be dealing with contracts. Futures contracts, alright? They trade in increments of 0.25. You don't mess up those decimals, or they'll eat you alive. Like this," Dave pointed out, scribbling something on a pad. "252.25, 301.00, 287.75, those are typical prices. The S&P index is trading between 125.00 and 375.00. So keep that in your head. You'll hear a lot of shouting, a lot of prices tossed around.

Your job? Listen and record. You'll be sending orders to brokers. They won't care if you're nervous or not."

"So, I just write down the prices when they yell out?"

"Exactly. And don't get distracted. The guys in the pit? They're here to make money. Don't look like you're in the way. Don't ask questions. Just follow the signals. If someone yells a price, make sure you know whether they're buying or selling, then find the other side of the trade and make sure it gets done. If you're not sure, ask. But do it quick and keep your head on a swivel."

I scribbled Dave's orders on my notepad. "What do I do if I mess up?"

Dave gave me a sharp look. "You don't mess up. If you do, you clean it up fast, and you take the heat. In this game, there are no second chances. Keep your records straight, your orders clear, and never stop moving. You make a mistake; you'll be eating it for a while. The brokers don't forget, and they'll hold it against you. You don't want that. Ever."

I nodded, swallowing hard. "Got it. But how do I know which broker to send stuff to?"

"Good question, but you better learn fast. You'll have to know who's who in the pit. Look for the ones with the red jackets, those are your guys. And don't make the mistake of approaching the power brokers unless you've got something big. Stick with the assistant brokers and work your way up. Don't be a hero on your first day."

He paused, looking me over. "One last thing, Michael, if you ever get caught not paying attention in that pit, you're done. They'll eat you alive. Don't get caught looking like a fool. This is a serious business. The Merc's not a place for slackers."

"Got it," I said, the warning in his words rang clear.

"Alright. Get in there, do your job, and keep your eyes wide open. Don't screw up, boy!" Dave shouted as his red jacket vanished into the swarm of neon.

"Hey, I miss the suit," Nora, the vixen Dave warned me about, whispered as she brushed past me. Her heels clicked against the cement floor of the pit. I barely looked up, keeping my head down as I wiped the sweat off my palms.

"Yeah, well, that was before I knew better," I muttered.

She laughed, the sound sharp and teasing. It wasn't the first time she'd commented on my transition from suit to clerk's jacket. Every time she saw me, it was a reminder that I was still finding my feet in this mess of chaos and noise. She paused just long enough to look over her shoulder at me.

"You're getting there, though. You've been at it for a few weeks now."

I shrugged, trying not to make a big deal of it. "Yeah, I'm still figuring it out."

Nora leaned in, her scent drifting over as she got close enough to speak quietly. "Don't let Owen make you think it's all easy. He's been at this forever. You're still new." I already knew Owen was in the game and winning. He was at home here, always had been.

"You should be making your own moves soon," she added with a sly grin. "You don't plan on just standing around forever, do you?"

I forced a tight smile. The truth was, I wasn't sure I was ready to make any moves.

"Trying to keep my head down for now. I don't want to mess it up."

"Good luck with that, I can practically see your palms itching to participate." She winked, then turned and I watched her weave through the crowd of traders in their bright jackets.

I adjusted my collar, still not used to how the jacket felt compared to the suit I had worn on my first day. *That* suit had been a mistake, and Dave had been right about one thing—it made me stand out, in a way I didn't want to. Now, weeks later, the jacket was my uniform, and I was getting used to it. Still, I didn't feel like I belonged here, not yet.

Not like Owen.

Owen was in the thick of it in the S&P 500 pit. He moved like he owned the place, shouting orders with ease and signaling trades with practiced gestures, while I stood on the sidelines trying to keep track of the chaos. Just as I was thinking about my friend's accomplishments, he walked into the pit. The trading floor began to buzz with energy, and I spotted his broad towering shoulders immediately, his blue jacket cutting through neon like a flag.

He was always one of the first to arrive, his confidence clear even in the chaos of the early morning grind. I'd been there for weeks now, always arriving early too. I longed to stay ahead of the curve, but I still felt like an outsider. Owen had been in the business long enough to move through the floor with ease.

"Morning, rookie," he tossed over his shoulder as he passed me with a playful grin on his face.

"Morning," I muttered, still wiping sweat from my palms as I tried to focus on the orders in front of me.

My job as a clerk was simple enough—write down the trades, keep track of the numbers—but it wasn't glamorous, and I couldn't help but notice the way brokers suspiciously eyed each other when a trade went through. Nevertheless, I learned to push away my curiosity and focus on proving myself. Owen settled into position, catching a few quick glances at the board, before shouting a bid across the pit. The sound of his voice carried above the shouting traders, his movements fast and decisive. It was clear he knew what he was doing.

"Did you see that move?" he asked, sidling up to me, grinning widely after a particularly tense round of bids. "I grabbed a few contracts at 127.75, sold them at 128.00. Quick profit." I tried to hide how much I envied the ease with which he traded. It wasn't just luck; it was skill.

Something I didn't have yet.

"What about you?" Owen asked, raising an eyebrow. "You're staring at the board like it's a foreign language."

I shrugged. "I'm just doing what you told me. Watching and learning."

Owen chortled lightly, "It's all about timing, Michael. You get that, you'll make your first trade. And trust me, when you do, it's gonna feel like a shot of adrenaline straight to the heart."

I scanned the pit. The chaos of the S&P 500 futures trading floor was a blur of colors, bodies shifting like a wave of stock market sea creatures. The clamor of voices, the gestures, the prices flashing on the board—it was starting to become familiar, but still, I wasn't quite sure I had it in me. I was a clerk, and that's all I'd been so far. The noise, the trading frenzy, it made me feel like I was on the outside looking in. Still, Owen's trade was impressive. I grabbed my pen and scribbled down the numbers with a sense of pride for my friend.

He made it look easy, but I knew it wasn't.

"What did Dave say again about standing out?" I asked, glancing at Owen for some reassurance.

"He said we can't afford to be quiet, to hide in the back," Owen replied. "You've got to shout if you want to get your trades in. You'll get the hang of it."

I wasn't so sure.

Watching the others, I could see the traders in constant motion, how they maneuvered their bodies and voices, calling bids over the din. It was a rhythm, an energy I was unsure that I could match. But Owen was right about one thing: timing was the key to it all.

"Let's see what today brings," I said, trying to shake off the doubt.

Owen's eyes glinted with that typical trader confidence. "If you've learned anything from watching, today might just be your day."

"What do you mean?" I asked my friend. He smiled slyly, and I knew he was up to something.

"Come on, Mike," Owen said, his voice low but eager. "You've been watching long enough. Time for you to make a move."

I froze for a second. "I'm just a clerk, Owen. You know that. I don't know how to make a trade, not really."

But he wasn't going to let me off the hook. "You've been writing down orders, right? You know how it works. Just give me a number. Look at the screen, tell me what you see. You can't screw this up."

I hesitated, but he looked at me with determination. I wasn't sure if I was more nervous about the trade or the risk of making a mistake and costing him money. But I'd watched him do it enough that something inside me told me to try.

What was the worst that could happen?

I glanced at the board, trying to make sense of it. The S&P 500 futures were showing at 130.25 for the bid and 130.50 for the ask, with some trades happening in between. I felt my heart rate increase as I saw the flux in prices.

"Buy at 130.25," I said, not completely sure of myself but trying to sound confident.

Owen leaned in, nodding with approval. "Good. Now watch the screen. It might take a minute, but don't blink."

I watched, heart pounding, as the screen flickered and refreshed. Seconds felt like hours, but then the price moved to 130.50. I grabbed a piece of paper, scrawled it down, and looked at Owen.

"Sell at 130.50," I said, my voice barely above a whisper. Owen gave me a sly grin, then turned back to the pit and shot his hand into the air. His fingers formed a quick "buy" signal, palm facing in, fingers bent slightly, a move I'd seen him use countless times.

"Buy at 130.25," he called, his voice cutting through the chaos. A moment later, he flipped his palm outward, signaling a sale. "Sell at 130.50," he bellowed with equal confidence before he turned toward me.

"See, Mike? A quick trade. Now, you've got the hang of it!" A jolt of excitement shot through me as I wrote it down. It wasn't a big trade, just a few contracts, but the rush I got from seeing the price shift in our favor was real.

"You feel that, Mike?" Owen's voice was barely audible over the noise. "That's the rush. That's what gets you hooked." I nodded as I embraced the adrenaline.

"You just made money, Mike!" Owen hooted from the pit. "And we didn't screw it up. That's a win." He flashed a charming smile, then turned back to the pit, already searching for his next move.

I held the paper with the details of the trade, feeling the weight of realization settle in. It was a small victory, but a victory, nonetheless. It wasn't just about the money; it was the adrenaline everyone had talked about for weeks. I never really believed it until I felt it for myself. The noise and chaos of the trading pit faded with the passing hours. The sudden sound of the bell signaled the end of the day and the traders around me started to wind down as they gathered their things and exchanged quick words about their day's wins or losses. My job as a clerk wasn't done yet, though.

I pulled out my trading cards, reviewing the paper trades I had written down throughout the day. Accuracy was key. Every contract, every price, had to be precise. I double-checked the small trade I had made with Owen earlier. He'd grabbed a few contracts and sold them quickly which I wrote down and reviewed one last time. As I was about to finish up, I noticed a few murmurs among the traders.

Out of the corner of my eye, I saw Lenny Gadsen, one of the big power brokers, talking to a clerk in the back. There was nothing unusual about it, except the clerk seemed overly jittery, nodding nervously as Lenny spoke. I decided not to read too much into it, it wasn't my business, but curiosity gnawed at me.

Just do your job and go home.

Owen's warning echoed through my mind, causing my attention to shift immediately back to my orders. I finished confirming the trades and began to hand them into the desk. The pit was nearly empty now, the frantic energy of the day replaced by the slow rhythm of clerks finishing up their duties. I was just about done when I heard a voice behind me.

"You made a move today, huh?" Dave's voice was low but steady.

I turned to face him, trying to keep my composure. "Yeah. Small paper trade with Owen. Nothing big."

He raised an eyebrow, giving me a small nod of approval. "You've been watching, learning. It's good to see you taking it seriously."

I swallowed hard. "It's just one trade, Dave."

He waved a hand, dismissing my humility. "Doesn't matter if it's small. You're starting to think like a trader. A couple more weeks, and I think you'll be ready to make your own moves. Just keep your eyes open and keep learning. Don't rush it. You've got the right instincts, but timing is everything. Make sure you're ready when the time comes."

I nodded, a mix of relief and excitement coursing through me. "Thanks, Dave. I'm just trying to keep up."

He gave me a sharp look. "You're doing fine, Michael. Don't let the noise distract you and focus on the work."

He turned and walked off, leaving me to wrap up my final tasks for the day. I stared at the piles of customer orders, the weight of the pen in my hand reminding me of how much I still had to learn. The idea of trading on my own still felt distant—almost like a dream—but after today, I was confident I could make it happen.

CHAPTER THREE

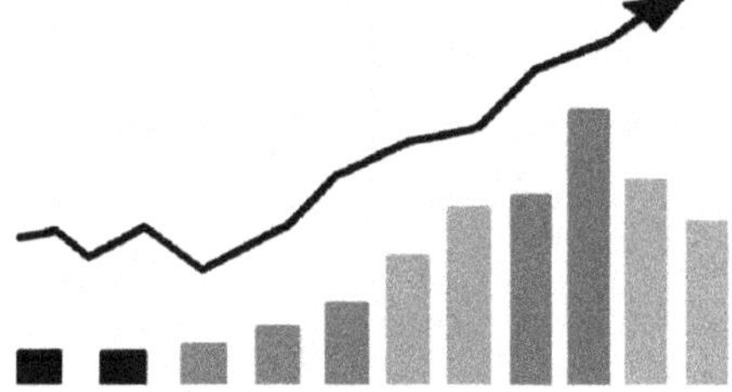

The bell rang, its sharp clang cutting through the air like a shot. The chaos erupted immediately.

"Let's go, let's go!" A man beside me shoved past, his trading cards clutched tightly in one hand. "Buy at 135.00, sell at 135.25.!" His voice was raw and desperate. I glanced around. Hands shot into the air, fingers signaling quantities and prices in a chaotic yet deliberate rhythm, each gesture an urgent bid for attention. The shouting was deafening.

"Five at135.25.25! A man in a mustard-colored jacket bellowed, his voice cutting through the din. His eyes darted toward me, sharp and expectant, as if I might hold the answer he was looking for.

"Sell! Sell now!" someone screamed, and I could feel the weight of the pressure to not be the last one standing still.

A thick cloud of expensive cologne wafted by, mixing with the sharp tang of sweat. The scent of freshly brewed coffee lingered in the air, along with the dry, musty smell of old paper. It all hit me at once, a suffocating mixture that only added to the madness. My senses buzzed; every inch of my skin felt alive with the frenetic energy around me.

"Ten contracts at 136.75! A man on my right yelled. He was wearing a pinstriped yellow jacket that practically screamed for attention. His eyes darted between the screen and me.

The movement was quick, fast, and it felt like the world blurred around me but my mind was calm. Focused. Someone bumped into me, their shoulder colliding with mine.

"Watch it, newbie!" the guy grunted, brushing past, his oversized coat billowing out like a cape as he charged toward the next deal.

"Watch your back, man," another growled, "or you'll get steamrolled." The sea of faces made it hard to identify who was speaking. I took a breath as the adrenaline of the pit filled me. The numbers on the screen flickered, shifting in real time, but I couldn't afford to blink.

I have to keep up, have to quickly learn the game.

"Goddamn, it's like a war zone in here," someone muttered nearby. His voice was barely audible over the din, but I caught the frustration in his tone. "Can't get a word in edgewise."

"Buy it up! Buy it now!" a man in a bright red coat shouted, his tinny voice cut through the others like a knife.

"What's the price?" someone asked urgently.

"Twenty at seventy-five!" he barked back, without missing a beat.

I felt the rush then, the way everything seemed to move faster the longer you stayed in the same spot. Testosterone and adrenaline hung thick in the air. The shouting, the deals, the hustle. It was all the same. One big, chaotic rush.

"Sell at twenty-two!" someone screamed, and I could feel my heart race, my mind working through the figures.

This was it. The energy was intoxicating, like it had always been in the locker rooms back when I was playing football. Everyone pushing, yelling, and clawing for the win. Sports and trading went hand in hand.

"Who's got a price on thirty-five?" The question brought me back.

After a week of experience in the pit, I didn't feel like just a face in the crowd anymore. The initial confusion of stepping into this maelstrom had faded. I had found my rhythm, my space, and now, standing on the trading floor, I felt almost at home. The crowd around me didn't feel so intimidating anymore. It was just another game. An opportunity, yes, but a game all the same. Dave's voice echoed in my mind, cutting through the chaos.

"Don't get caught up in the noise, Michael," he had said to me just yesterday. His eyes were sharp behind his gray glasses. He'd looked at me like I was a kid trying to play in a man's game. "The floor's full of noise. People yelling, prices changing, deals flying around. It'll mess with your head if you let it. You can't listen to every shout. You've gotta tune out the distractions. Focus on the screens. The numbers tell you everything you need to know. If you're not looking at the right data, you're already losing." Now, in the thick of it, I knew exactly what he meant.

"Hey! You got this, kid!" the obese man beside me yelled, his voice booming over the noise. His oversized purple checkered jacket swelled with each shout. Spit flew from his mouth, landing in the air between us.

I winced, but I didn't flinch.

"Focus, focus, focus," I muttered under my breath, keeping my eyes locked on the screens.

"Don't get distracted!" he shouted again. Right after that, Owen's voice pierced through the chaos, low and sharp, like a warning.

"Don't listen to him," he said as he appeared beside me. His face was tight, his eyes scanned the screen and he spoke quickly. "It's all part of the show. Don't let anyone get in your head. Not even the ones who act like they're your buddy."

I glanced at him. "What do you mean? The guy's just trying to help."

Owen shook his head, eyes narrowing on the trading floor. "No. He's trying to distract you. Don't let anyone make you think they're on your side. They're not. Not here. It's all a game and if you show any weakness, you're toast. You've got to be a wall, not a sponge."

I frowned, not fully understanding, but I could see the truth in Owen's expression. It wasn't just about numbers on a screen; it was about your individuality. There were no friends in trading.

"You really think so, huh?" I asked.

Owen didn't look at me directly, his voice steady as he answered. "Yes, trust no one. Everyone's got their own angle. The friendly ones, the ones who pretend they're helping? They want you to slip up. They want to catch you off guard so they can take advantage of you. It's about survival out here. So keep your head down and stay sharp. You'll see the truth when no one claps for your victories and everyone laughs at your failures."

I opened my mouth to argue, but thought better of it. I just wanted to trade and didn't care much about making friends. I looked back at the screen, the numbers flashing in front of me and ticking away.

"Alright," I said, my voice quieter now. "I'll trust no one."

Owen gave a nod of approval. "Good. And remember, no one's your friend here, not even me." He slapped me on the back and moved away, getting lost in the sea of chaos again.

I tried to block out the noise around me. The obese man was still shouting, but his words weren't reaching me anymore. I was locked in. It reminded me of those days back on the football field. The rush of competition. The way the crowd would roar, the opposing players shouting and grunting with every move. Back then, I'd been a quarterback; feeling the weight of the game in my hands, trusting my instincts, making decisions in a split second, just like now. I grinned at the memory. My heart raced in the same way now, my pulse quickening as I moved with the crowd, trying to stay one step ahead.

I straightened my yellow jacket, a surge of pride washing over me. This jacket was mine, my symbol of belonging on the trading floor. It wasn't just fabric and stitching; it was a reminder of how far I'd come and the role I now played in the chaos of the pit. As I looked at it, a new sense of confidence settled in. I could handle this.

I belonged here.

"Motherfucker!" A burly man cussed loudly.

A fight broke out on the floor and fists flew left and right. Noses were shattered and the blood stains stood out on their yellow jackets. Security sauntered over with no sense of emergency and the two fuming men were escorted out of the building. The fat man next to me chortled loudly and I could smell his breath, thick with the sour scent of cigarettes. He had that eager look on his face, the one that told me he enjoyed the chaos.

Owen was right.

The floor buzzed around me, but I stayed calm. My eyes were locked on the screens, watching the numbers tick by like clockwork, every digit telling a story.

"Hey, handsome." Nora was pressed against me, her lips inches from my ear. "You can't just stand there and stare at the screens, you gotta be talking and moving. If you're quiet, you'll lose out."

I didn't answer. She swung her hips as she walked away but I couldn't afford to get distracted. I wasn't here to talk or socialize. I was here to make money, to make my move. I wasn't like the rest of these guys who shouted at each other, all bluster and noise. Experience showed me this wasn't about the loudest voice but about reading the room, reading the screens, the patterns, and the flow of the market.

I could feel the tension building, the heat of the moment. The trading floor felt like a living, breathing organism, every movement, every shout, and every gesture was calculated. But I wasn't overwhelmed by it anymore. I was in control. I could feel the pressure and it didn't scare me. It excited me.

This was the moment. I was able to get a chance to now get a chance to trade for the brokerage firm that I worked for with a small account that they had set up for me and I was now on my way. I felt had had done enough paper trades to give it a go and since it was their money at risk, what did I have to lose. The process took about a week, but I was now ready to venture into the pit and swim with the sharks,

My eyes flicked over the figures on the screen, calculating, assessing, weighing my options. The markets were moving fast, faster than I'd ever seen, but I had learned to trust my instincts.

In an instant, I called out, "Sell 5 contracts at 152.25!"

The words left my mouth before I had even fully processed them, but somehow, I knew it was right. My heart pounded as I waited for the response. I wasn't looking for anyone's approval. I just needed to know if I was right, if this decision would pay off. The tension held for a heartbeat, then another, then finally.

"Buy it!" someone shouted back, and just like that, my trade was set.

I stood still for a moment as the floor spun around me. I couldn't hear anything except the pounding of my own heart. The din between trades felt deafening as I waited for the numbers to fall into place. My mind raced, calculating the potential gains. A few seconds passed, but it felt like a lifetime. The numbers continued to flicker on the screen and a rush of disbelief surged through me. My stomach dropped.

Approximately $3000 on one trade.

I couldn't believe it. The figures were there, but my mind couldn't quite catch up with the reality. I'd done it. I had actually done it. I scanned the floor, catching Owen's eyes across the chaos. His face lit up when he saw my first trade go through, and in an instant, he was pushing his way through the crowd, making a beeline for me.

"Holy shit, Mike!" Owen yelled over the shouts of men. "You did it!" He laughed, his grin spreading wide. "You're not a rookie anymore. That was smooth as hell."

I grinned back, but it felt strange, almost surreal. The adrenaline was still coursing through me, but my mind was struggling to catch up. 3000 dollars. Just like that. It was hard to wrap my head around.

"Yeah," I muttered, still trying to process. "I guess I am."

The weight of it all started to settle in like a brick dropping in my stomach. But there was something else there too. A rush. A high. The kind that made my pulse quicken. I could feel it spreading, the recognition of what I'd just done. I wasn't just some guy in the crowd anymore. I was one of them. A player.

"We're celebrating this weekend, huh?" Dave's voice was loud and unmistakable in the middle of the hubbub. I hadn't even noticed his arrival. "First round's on me!"

I laughed, overjoyed by my win and still trying to make sense of the feeling in my chest. A celebration sounded good, but I couldn't stop thinking about the trade. The numbers. The decision. It was like a fire had been lit in me. I wasn't just standing here, lost in the euphoria that accompanied a successful trade.

I took a risk, and I'd earned this reward.

"Hell yeah, we're celebrating!" I said, struggling to suppress the grin that tugged at the corners of my mouth. I was still buzzing from the high of my first successful trade. It was all I could think about.

I'm not just a rookie anymore. I'm playing the game. And the ball is in my court.

As Owen and Dave planned the weekend's celebrations, and I still tried to absorb everything, I caught sight of Seth Kaufman. He wasn't a trader, but everyone knew him. He looked like George Washington, right down to the powdered wig.

Well, not in a literal sense.

But his whole vibe screamed 18th century, with his ridiculous coat that he wore after hours. It looked like it was made for a colonial general. Everyone always laughed about it, but no one dared say it to his face. Seth had a way of moving through the room like a predator. His gaze lingered too long, like he was devising ways to ruin you, and no one wanted to test that. He nodded as he passed by me, a slow, deliberate acknowledgment. It wasn't the kind of nod you gave a friend. It was one of those looks that made the hairs on the back of your neck stand up, a silent reminder that nothing went unnoticed. It was a message that left a chill in its wake.

"Good one," he sneered, his voice low and dry. He didn't break stride, but his words felt heavy, as if they carried more weight than simple praise. I forced a smile as unease coiled in my gut.

Was it genuine acknowledgment or a warning? With Seth, you never really knew.

My mind replayed every second of the trade, every flicker of Seth's expression. Whatever his intentions, I couldn't dwell on it.

I did it. I made my mark.

The energy of the floor that once overwhelmed me now drove me forward. But Seth's nod lingered in the back of my mind, a reminder that for every win, eyes were always watching and calculating.

For what? I didn't know.

"You're making it to the top. One step at a time. How does it feel, man?" Owen's question pulled me back to reality.

I laughed, shaking my head and holding onto the buzz of winning. "Not bad at all."

Owen gave me a firm congratulatory handshake before taking his leave.

But staying on top? That was an entirely different game.

CHAPTER FOUR

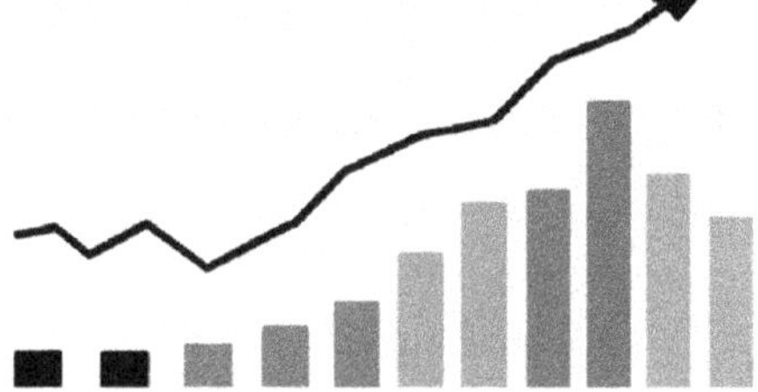

Spilled alcohol soaked the carpeted bus floor, mixing with the sharp scent of sweat and expensive cologne. The stale air clung to the cramped space as the bus swerved through the crowded streets of Chicago. The music pounded so hard it reverberated through my bones, and for a moment I could barely make out the faces around me. Everyone had shed their uniform jackets, now dressed in sleek outfits for a night of escape. The floor was a blur of well-dressed strangers, all immersed in the pulse of the night—a stark contrast to the chaos of the pit.

"Mr. Russo!" Will's gravelly voice sliced through the chaos.

He swaggered toward me, his presence impossible to ignore. Will was larger than life, the kind of guy everyone knew by reputation. A power broker by day, a drugged-up party animal by night, and always at the center of every scene. He clapped a hand on my shoulder, a gesture I've come to realize was a common way of greeting. A flash of white teeth shone in the dim light of the bus as Will smiled expectantly.

"Well, well, well, if it isn't the star of the show!" he bellowed. "I've been hearing all kinds of things about you, Russo. Young trader quickly rising to the top, huh? You're really making a name for yourself." I was unsure how to feel about catching the eye of Will Lawrence. He leaned closer, the smell of whiskey and stale cigarettes drifting from his smart clothes.

"So tell me, what's your magic formula, huh?" he asked curiously.

"Educated guesses," I said flatly, hoping to deflect the conversation. Will raised an eyebrow, clearly unimpressed by my nonchalant response. He leaned back and took a slow drag from his drink, his calculating gaze piercing into me the entire time.

"Educated guesses, huh?" he repeated, quieter now, and more probing. "You don't look like the guessing type, Michael. There's gotta be more to it than that. You're not playing the game the way the rest of us do."

I forced a smile and kept my cool. Confidence had been the key lesson I'd learned in my time on the trading floor.

"Maybe I'm just lucky," I said, my tone final.

Will chuckled, his eyes narrowed slightly as if weighing my every word. The air between us was tense as we both sipped our drinks and glared at each other. I could almost feel the wheels turning in his head.

"Sure, kid," he finally said, his tone shifting back to its usual boisterous self, but there was a flicker of doubt in his eyes. He leaned in again, and I wanted to back away, but the dancing bodies behind me kept me in place.

"Anyway, I came here to ask you, what's your poison?" His breath reeked as he stared at me with a devilish grin.

This man is a walking paradox.

I looked him up and down. He wore an off-the-rack suit that didn't quite match the energy of the night, but the way he carried himself made it work. His shirt was untucked, sleeves rolled up, a cocktail in hand, and as he lingered in my space the scent of something stronger than alcohol wafted around him.

"I'm good for now." I raised my beer and Will eyed it humorously. He laughed, and the sound rumbled through the bus.

"Come on, you can't be all work and no play. I know what you're doing in that suit, Russo. Trying to look all serious, all business. But you're in my world now. And in my world, we drink, we smoke, we snort, we swallow, and we fuck. So tell me, boy, what's your poison? First time is on the house." He winked slyly.

I hesitated and felt the pressure to engage in a deal with the devil himself. Will's reputation alone made him someone you didn't turn down. I couldn't shake the feeling that being around him might make or break whatever I was trying to do here. Will waited patiently, his expression a mix of expectation and amusement. It was clear he wasn't going anywhere until he got an answer. I touched the tip of my nose with a shaky finger, and a hint of mischief lit up in his slanted eyes.

"That's my boy!" he hollered.

I looked around nervously to see if anyone was watching as he grabbed a nearby table and, with a small grunt, shakily pulled it closer. Settling into our seats opposite each other, he fumbled around in his inside pockets and pulled out a small plastic packet. The white powder stood out under the dim lights of the bus, and my stomach tightened with a knot of dread. Regret started to gnaw at my insides as he spread it across the table. My mind screamed, but the party raged on around me, louder and faster, as Will expertly cut through the contents with a credit card.

"You know what to do with this?" he asked with anticipation.

"No," I said honestly.

His grin widened as he took out a crisp hundred-dollar bill, rolled it up with practiced ease, and leaned over the table. Then, with a dramatic flourish, he bent down and snorted a line before sitting back up abruptly, red-faced, with powder scattered across his nose.

"Whoo!" he shouted, nearly knocking over his drink. "That's how you do it! Go ahead, boy! What you waiting for?"

He handed me the rolled-up bill, and for a second, I froze. The weight of the moment pressed down on me, and my hand hovered over the contents.

This was it, an invitation to a new world ...

Before I could lean toward the table, a firm hand grabbed my shoulder and stopped me.

"Not so fast," Dave's interruption made me sigh in relief. His voice was low but it carried through the noise. "Sharing is caring, you know?" He winked before sliding next to me. As his body blocked the view of Will and the table Dave shot me a quick, almost imperceptible glance.

"Dave, my man! You know I always got supply for you!" Will began another search through his deep, hidden pockets. While he was distracted, Dave leaned in closer to me.

"You don't want to do that," he whispered. I looked at him, confused, but before I could respond, he took the hundred from my hand in a swift motion. "I'll take that," he said with a sly smile, slipping it into his pocket. Will was too caught up lining up the powdered contents.

Dave, with a nonchalant grin, snorted the cocaine instead. I realized that he was saving me, but in his own twisted way as he was still part of the mess. The line of powder vanished, and Dave wiped his nose with the back of his hand, looking perfectly casual as if nothing had happened. Before I could protest, Owen appeared and cut through the crowd like a linebacker on the move. On his arm was a beautiful blonde with long legs who, somehow, walked steadily on the shaky bus.

"There's the man of the hour!" He grabbed me by the arm with a force that made me stumble slightly.

"Come on, Mikey," he said, dragging me and the pretty lady toward the back of the bus. "I've got someone I want you to meet. You're gonna love her!"

I couldn't even process the words; my mind still spun from the close call with Will's offer. Owen's grip tightened as he pulled me through the writhing bodies, and I let myself be swept along, barely aware of the faces we passed or the drinks being sloshed about.

"Who is she?" I managed to ask, trying to keep up.

"A real catch," he replied with a wink, his expression all mischievous delight. "You'll see."

We pushed our way through the throngs of people towards the back, where a woman sat on a raised booth. She had fiery red hair that fell in unruly curls over her petite shoulders. Her hazel eyes seemed to look straight through me as I maneuvered through the dancing crowd. She was dressed in a black suit that made her stand out from the women in dresses. Something about her didn't fit the environment, she looked powerful and mesmerizing.

"There she is!" Owen snapped me back to reality. "Shannon Clarke, this is Michael Russo. The man, the legend!" I blushed at Owen's praise as we stopped in front of her and Shannon stood up.

"Nice to meet you." Her voice was as silky as her hair. Her handshake was firm, yet soft. The perfect combination for the perfect woman. "Owen tells me you're making a name for yourself on the floor," she continued, leaning in slightly as the music pounded around us. Her lips barely moved, and I had to lean in closer to hear her words.

"Something like that," I replied, keeping my tone neutral as I scanned her face for any signs of insincerity. There were none. She was sharp. I could tell.

"Well, that's impressive," she said, studying me intently. "Not everyone can make it in that world." Her words hung in the air and felt real.

She wasn't just saying it because it was the polite thing to say. She wasn't trying to impress me, and that made her stand out even more. The intensity of the beat, the flashing lights, the noise—it all started to fade into the background as we talked.

"So, what about you?" I asked, genuinely curious. "What's your story?"

She chuckled softly, the sound sweeter than the cherries in our cocktails. "I'm just a woman who's trying to find my way in a man's world. I've always been more interested in... real conversations, you know?"

Finally, someone who didn't seem like a cardboard cut-out of the typical club-goer.

"I know exactly what you mean," I responded with a knowing smile. "So, what do you do?" I asked, trying to break through the noise.

"I'm a lawyer," she said passionately. "I work in corporate law mostly. It's challenging but rewarding." Her enthusiasm was clear. She leaned in slightly and her red hair brushed against my arm. "I love it. There's always something new, always a puzzle to solve. It's like a game, figuring out how to make everything fit."

I pictured her in a courtroom and smiled. "Sounds like a lot of strategy."

She laughed. "Yeah, but not the fun kind of strategy. It's all about making sure things don't fall apart. A lot of legal jargon, and a lot of paperwork, but I love it."

"You seem pretty into it," I said, genuinely impressed. "It's nice to see someone who actually enjoys their job."

"I'm lucky." She smiled softly. "A lot of people fall into jobs because they have to. I actually *chose* mine. But enough about me, what about you?"

I hesitated, unsure if I should tell her the full truth. "Well, I'm... still figuring it out. Been making some moves, you know? But it's all pretty new to me. Felt like a fish out of water when I first came into this scene."

She chuckled, her laughter easy and warm. "You? A fish out of water? I don't believe it!"

"I'm serious." I put on my best serious face and she laughed at my comical expression. "Jokes aside, the whole trading thing? It's like a whole other language. The noise, the chaos, it's insane. Everyone seems to know what they're doing, but me? I'm just trying not to drown in it."

She raised an eyebrow, clearly intrigued. "Really? You don't seem like you'd be the type to get lost in a crowd."

"I guess I hide it well," I said with a half-smile. "But it's a rush, you know?"

She studied me for a second, "I get it. It's all about the high, isn't it? That moment where you just know you made the right move, or maybe the wrong one. But you can't stop."

"Exactly," I said, grateful that she understood. "And the stakes are so high, you can't back down once you're in."

I let out a quiet laugh, surprised by how easily the conversation flowed between us. For someone who looked like she didn't belong in a place like this, she sure seemed comfortable in the chaos. By the time we reached the club, the night had started to feel like it could go on forever. The neon lights blinked ahead, drawing us in, and we stepped off the bus together, me keeping close to her side. Inside, the music was even louder, the crowd even more electric. It felt like a world of its own, buzzing with energy. But Shannon wasn't fazed. She seemed like she could walk into any room and own it.

"Dance with me?" I offered my hand confidently to her.

Shannon eyed my hand suspiciously but eventually gave in. We danced together, talked, and navigated through the crowd with the ease of two strangers becoming more.

"What is it about this place?" I asked as we sat at the bar. Shannon looked around at the sea of people dancing and shouting, her chest rising and falling rapidly as she caught her breath from all the dancing. Her expression shifted slightly before responding.

"A lot of people are here to escape," she said. "They come for the party, for the distraction. But it's not really what they need, you know? It's like they think if they keep moving they won't have to face whatever's waiting for them on the other side." I stared at her, struck by the truth in her words.

"Yeah, I get that," I said. A silence fell between us.

Eventually, Shannon checked her watch and sighed. "I should get going," she said, her tone tinged with reluctance. "Got work in the morning." The thought of her leaving felt like an unexpected tug.

"Yeah, I should probably go too." Though the idea of never seeing her again made me hesitate.

She smiled up at me. "It was nice talking to you, Michael. Really."

"You too," I said, feeling a strange sense of loss. "I'll... see you around?"

"Maybe," she said with a wink. "Here's my number, in case you ever want to talk." She handed me a small piece of paper with her number scrawled on it.

"Thanks," I said, unable to hide the excitement in my voice.

As she walked away with practiced grace, I knew this night with her would stick with me longer than I expected.

I should've kissed her. But it was too late as I watched her disappear into the crowd. I scanned the crowd for Dave and Owen when a conversation caught my ear.

"After-hours trading," Will's voice, low and urgent, cut through the noise.

My feet felt like they were glued to the floor as I spotted him in a dim corner, speaking with a shadow I couldn't put a face to. I inched closer, blending into the darkness, trying to make sense of what I just heard. Will glanced over his shoulder before leaning in, his body language tensed. Then, a single beam of light cut across them, and the man's face was revealed.

Lenny Gadsen.

Will and Lenny shook hands, sealing a deal. I slowly pulled back, the unease in my stomach settling like a stone.

I wasn't meant to witness this.

CHAPTER FIVE

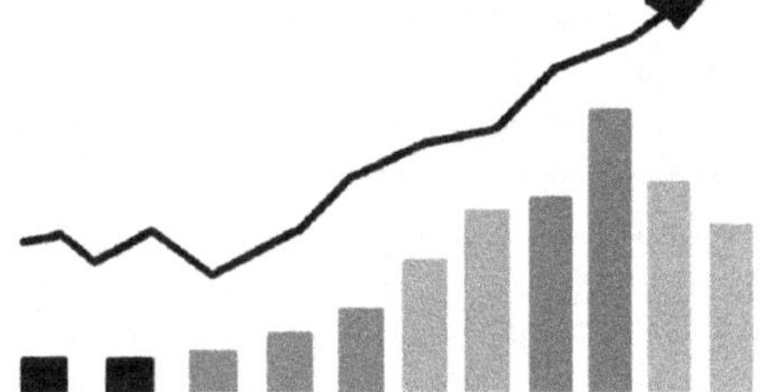

The roar of the crowd filled my ears as I sat with Vince, Steve, and Owen. All of us were on the edge of our seats at the Chicago Stadium, watching the Bulls take on the Detroit Pistons. The Bulls weren't pulling off the win tonight but, nevertheless, the atmosphere in the stadium was electric. Fans around us were decked out in Bulls red, shouting and cheering with all their might even as the Pistons in their white jerseys steadily pulled ahead.

"Get in there, Jordan!" Steve shouted. His voice struggled to cut through the noise. The men tried to stay optimistic, even when things were slipping away for the Bulls. The ball was in Michael Jordan's hands and the crowd's excitement swelled as he made his way down the court, dribbling smoothly and dodging Pistons defenders.

"Look at that move!" Owen hollered excitedly; his voice full of admiration. "He's going to be something special!"

"Just not tonight!" I yelled back.

Despite the Bulls' struggles, Jordan's talent was undeniable. Vince, seated next to me, was focused on the game in his usual quiet way. He wasn't much of a talker during the game, but I knew he was absorbing every detail, always calculating, always evaluating, whether it was on the court or in the pit. The scoreboard ticked down, the minutes slipping away as the Bulls failed to close the gap. With only seconds left, it was clear the game was all but over.

"Well, that's a wrap!" Vince sat back in his seat, shaking his head slightly as the crowd began to boo. "Tough game."

"Yeah," Steve said with a sigh, his optimism fading for the moment. "But hey, at least we got Jordan to look forward to."

"He put up quite a game, but Moncrief was unstoppable," I said, trying to shake off the disappointment.

Sure, the Bulls had taken a hit, but this was just one game in a long season. There'd be plenty more chances for redemption.

"We can't let a game like that ruin the night," Owen said through the lull of the crowd. "There's a spot nearby where we can grab a drink. Ever been to The Twin Anchors?"

I shook my head. "No, I haven't."

"Well, you're about to get a real taste of Chicago then," Owen grinned, nudging me as he stood. "Let's go."

We filed out of the stadium and the chill of the evening air hit us as we stepped onto the street. A year ago, I might have felt out of place walking with these guys but now, I felt like I belonged. I walked with confidence, knowing I had earned my place among them.

The Twin Anchors was just a short walk away, nestled in Old Town. The bar was a classic, its warm atmosphere welcoming us as we walked in. The scent of smoked barbecue and ribs filled the air, making my mouth water. The dim lights gave the place a cozy, relaxed feel and a sense that this wasn't just a restaurant; it was a piece of the city's soul, where locals gathered to unwind after a long day. It was the complete opposite of the nightlife shenanigans we got up to with the rest of the trading gang. We grabbed a table and ordered drinks, the clink of glass against glass punctuating the air as Owen signaled the bartender.

"I'll take a whiskey ," Vince said, settling into his seat. "You?" he asked, glancing at me.

"A beer, thanks," I replied.

"Same for me," Owen added, pushing an empty glass to the side.

Steve smiled, raising his hand. "I'll go with a gin and tonic, something refreshing after that shitty game."

As the bartender walked away, I leaned back, letting the warmth of the place settle over me. I looked around at my friends, and a sense of gratitude washed over me. I had been the rookie a couple years ago on the trading floor but after meeting these guys I'd learned so much from them. They taught me more than just trading; they showed me how to read people, make decisions under pressure, and hold my ground in a world that could chew you up and spit you out.

"Here's to the Bulls," Vince said, raising his glass, the optimism in his voice still lingering despite the loss.

"To the Bulls," Steve and Owen echoed dully as we lifted our glasses with half-smiles.

The beer was cold, crisp, and just what I needed after the Bulls' loss tonight. It had a clean finish that seemed to wash away the disappointment of the day. As I took another satisfying sip the door of the bar creaked open, and suddenly the room filled with noise. Brad Coleman walked in with his usual confident presence and booming voice. He was one of our most fiery independent traders with a mouth as dirty as a dumpster.

"Well, well, well, look who's fuckin' here!" he called out and sauntered over to the jukebox with an ease that suggested he had come here a million times before. He smacked the side of the machine and punched a button. Rock music instantly filled the quiet space as he turned around and his eyes caught ours.

"There they are, my favorite traders!"

"Brad!" Owen called out, grinning from ear to ear. "You always know how to make a grand entrance."

Brad slapped the table and slid into the chair next to me. "Jackie! Another round for my boys!" he yelled, waving to the bartender who nodded.

"The usual for you, Coleman?" Jackie shouted back from behind the bar.

"Yes, my man! You know what I like." Brad winked at the bartender as a fresh round of beers was being prepared for us. He leaned back in his chair. "Man, I thought we had that game. Close, right? But hey, close only counts in horseshoes and hand grenades!"

Owen laughed, shaking his head. "Brad, you're like the unofficial ambassador of silver linings."

"What can I say? Life's too short to mope about a bad game."

Steve raised his glass. "I'll drink to that. And to a better season next year."

"Amen," Vince muttered, tilting his glass before taking a sip.

Brad turned to me. "Mike, come on, man, you've been quiet. Don't tell me you're still sulking over the game?"

I shrugged, smirking. "Nah, I'm just waiting for the next time the Bulls actually show up to play."

Brad laughed and grabbed my shoulder. "There he is! That's the Mike I know." He slid a fresh glass of beer toward me. "Drink up Mikey, we got the whole night before us."

Drinking and roughhousing was the normal lifestyle of an independent trader, and I was still getting used to it. The bar's jukebox switched to another classic rock hit, and Brad tapped his foot to the beat.

"This is a vibe. See? All you need is good music, cold beer, and decent company to turn the night around."

"But a Bulls win would've been nice," Vince interjected dryly.

"Details, details," Brad waved dismissively. "I'm telling you, next season is ours. Just wait."

We all leaned back comfortably, sipping our drinks as the buzz of conversation swirled around the bar. Brad eyed a waitress walking by with a tray of drinks. He nudged me, smirking. "Mike, take a look. That's prime Chicago right there."

I rolled my eyes, chuckling. "Brad, I'm good."

Owen leaned in with a sly smile pulling at the corner of his mouth. "Don't bother, Brad. Mike's got tunnel vision for Shannon. You'd have better luck convincing him to short S&P futures at the opening bell."

The table erupted in laughter, and Brad threw his hands up. "All right, all right! But come on, Mike, give us the details. What's the story with this Shannon?"

I hesitated, feeling the familiar warmth of embarrassment creep up. "She's amazing," I admitted. "Smart, funny, kind. And, yeah, I'm hooked."

"Aww!" came the loud chorus from the table. I could feel the stares from nearby patrons as they caught on to our laughter.

Vince raised his glass again. "Here's to Shannon, then. Sounds like you've got yourself a good one, Mike."

"Cheers to that," Brad added, clinking his glass against mine. "A rare find indeed, my man."

Owen's expression turned thoughtful. "You know Mike, finding someone you can trust—someone who's got your back no matter what—that's something you don't let go of."

Steve smiled, his gaze suddenly far away. "Yeah, I know that feeling. My wife, Cynthia, she's my rock. I love her more than anything. Although, she scares me sometimes. I fear for my life every day—and especially tonight. I'm gonna pay for it later," Steve added with a laugh. "Told her I'd be home right after the game, and now I'm stuck here with you bastards."

The table cracked up while Brad lifted his drink shakily. "Here's to Steve's last day on Earth!" They roared with laughter again as they cheered. Beer spilled everywhere and the bar came to life as the night progressed.

"Speaking of trust." Brad smacked the table and leaned in conspiratorially. "Do you guys trust our brokers back at the Merc?"

Our laughter slowly died down and every head at the table snapped toward him. The shift in tone was immediate, as if Brad had tossed a match into a dry brush and set fire to the place.

"What do you mean?" Vince asked cautiously, his gaze narrowing.

Brad shrugged, taking a sip of his beer. "Just saying, I've heard some things. Figured I'd see what you guys think."

The tension was palpable, and it seemed like the night's lighthearted energy had taken a sudden, serious turn.

Vince raised an eyebrow, Owen's smile faded, and Steve paused with his drink halfway to his lips. I could feel the sudden shift in the air.

"Well, do you?" Brad pressed, leaning back again, his grin still present but tinged with something sharper.

The mood at the table shifted from camaraderie to tension. My stomach knotted. I sipped my beer, letting the crisp taste distract me for a moment before the weight of the conversation pulled me back.

"I don't know," Vince finally said, breaking the silence. He leaned forward, resting his elbows on the table. "Lenny's been a broker for what, five years? That house in Winnetka? It's not just big, it's fucking excessive. Even at his best, I don't see how he's pulling in that kind of cash without something extra."

Steve nodded, his preppy demeanor unusually serious. "And Will's Porsche. It's not just about the car; it's the timing. He's suddenly throwing money around like it's burning a hole in his pocket. Makes you wonder if they've got more going on than we're seeing. And the drugs and partying almost every weekend? That doesn't sit right with me."

I glanced at Owen, who was still quiet, his expression unreadable. My mind churned as I recalled that night at the club. Lenny and Will had been hunched over their drinks, talking in low voices about "after-hours trades." I didn't understand it then, but the way they spoke it wasn't the casual banter of guys cutting loose. It felt... suspicious.

I cleared my throat. "There was this time," I began hesitantly. "At the club, last year. Lenny and Will were talking about after-hours deals.

It didn't make much sense to me at the time, but now... I don't know. It just felt shady."

Vince frowned. "Why didn't you say anything?"

I glanced nervously at Owen, the memory of his warnings flashed in my mind. He had told me to stay out of it, to keep my head down and focus on my own trades. I expected him to wave me off again, but instead, he leaned forward, his voice low and deliberate.

"You're not wrong, Mike," he said. "I've seen things too. Last week, I spotted Seth, the bagman, meeting up with one of the brokers after hours. It wasn't casual. They didn't even try to be discreet."

My pulse quickened at Owen's admission. If even he was starting to see cracks in the system, it meant this wasn't just paranoia, it was real.

Steve tapped his fingers on the table, his brow furrowed in deep thought. "Seth's not exactly known for his transparency. If he's involved, this could be bigger than we think."

Brad grimaced, but his eyes were sharp. "Bigger? You bet it is. You think Lenny's house and Will's car are just coincidences? There's a whole network under the surface, and it's dirty. I've seen enough to know."

Vince tilted his head. "And what are you suggesting Brad? It's not like we can do anything, we're just the traders."

Brad leaned in, his smirk widened as his voice dropped to a near whisper, dripping with intrigue. "What I'm saying is this: I'm sure there are other traders, guys like us, who've had enough. Real traders who are sick of watching the corruption eat away at this place. And it's about time we put an end to it. What's going on out there, it's bigger than any one of us. We can ignore it, let it slide, or we can step up."

The table went silent as we realized that he wasn't just passing along gossip; he was inviting us into something bigger.

"This kind of thing... it doesn't come without risks. Is it worth it?" I asked quietly.

Brad looked at each of us, his gaze unflinching. "Nothing worth doing comes without risks. But this? Whether you know it or not, this is hitting all of us at this table."

Steve's brow furrowed and his voice was edged with worry. "How? How is this affecting *us*?"

Brad laughed bitterly. "You think you're not affected? Every time a broker holds a customer order you get affected. Think about your money, your well-earned money. Some shitty broker decides to play both sides, every time they trade against their clients, guess who pays the price? We do. That's *our* profit disappearing into their pockets."

A chill ran through me. The implications of his words settled heavily in my mind.

"Jesus," Vince muttered, his face darkening. "I didn't think it was cutting into *our* trades."

Brad spread his hands. "That's what I'm saying. If you care about your trades, your future, and your reputation then we can't just sit back anymore. I don't know about you gentlemen but I'm done settling for less. I want the whole cake or none at all!" He chugged his beer as we took in what he said.

Owen said nothing while Vince and Steve exchanged uneasy glances but my interest was piqued. I looked at the fear in my friends and fellow traders' averted eyes and made a decision.

"Tell us more." The words were out, sealing my fate. Brad smiled wickedly and slammed his beer down, wiping the foam from his mouth with the back of his hand in one swift motion.

"I knew there was a fighting spirit in you, Mikey!" he exclaimed. "But first, tell me what you know about dual trading."

CHAPTER SIX

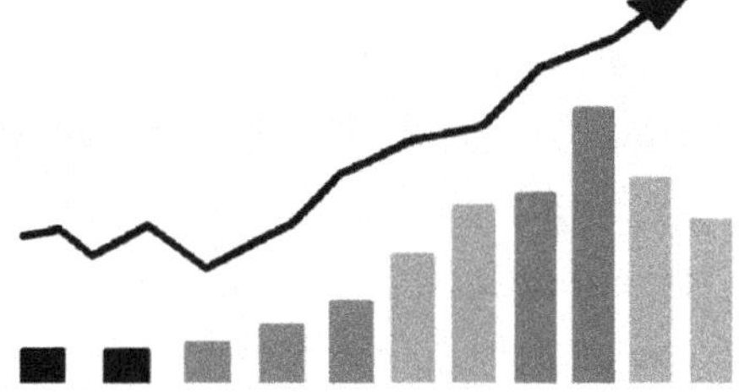

Shannon's red hair fanned out across the white linen, a fiery contrast to my apartment's cool light. I laid there, propped up on my elbow, unable to look away. She looked so peaceful as her chest rose and fell with each slow breath. Apart from her striking beauty, Shannon's passion for her job captivated me and her independence was even more attractive. She loved the law as much as I loved the market.

In moments like this, it was hard to reconcile the chaos of my world with the calm she brought. We'd been sneaking around for nights such as this, snatching stolen hours away from prying eyes. We lived in our own bubble, away from numbers and legislation, but she didn't deserve the secrecy or the shadows I dragged her into. Shannon deserved the world. And I was planning to give it to her when the time was right.

We came a long way in a short amount of time.

I remembered the way Shannon's hand trembled slightly in mine as we approached my parents' front door. She'd laughed nervously, brushing her fiery hair back, whispering, *"It's too soon, what if they don't like me?"* I'd reassured her, but honestly, I was more nervous than I let on. Shannon wasn't just anyone, she was *the one.*

The door opened, and my mom greeted us with her usual warmth, enveloping Shannon in a hug before I could even introduce her properly. Dad followed, more reserved but polite, his eyes assessing her. Over dinner, Shannon charmed them with stories of her relentless fights for her clients. She made even the driest legal anecdotes sound riveting, and by dessert, Mom was laughing so hard tears streamed down her cheeks and Dad gave me a subtle nod of approval.

Later, as we left, Shannon squeezed my hand.

"They're wonderful," she had said. And I knew they thought the same about her.

My eyes flicked to the chair by the window, where my coat hung. In the pocket was a small box, its weight far greater than its size. I'd imagined so many ways to give it to her, but this wasn't it. It had to be perfect, as perfect as she was. My thoughts shifted, unbidden, to the trading floor. To the bar. To Brad's words about dual trading. They had lingered with me all night, unsettling truths tangled with unspoken fears. Vince had voiced what we were all thinking, but it was Owen's quiet presence that had spoken volumes.

Could this system be bleeding us all dry? And more importantly, could I walk into the storm Brad hinted at?

Shannon stirred beside me, breaking my reverie. Her emerald eyes fluttered open, locking onto mine. A soft, sleepy smile curved her lips, and my heart ached at the sight.

"Morning, handsome," she murmured huskily.

"Morning, beautiful." I leaned in to kiss her forehead.

She stretched lazily and her fingers brushed against my arm. "You look deep in thought," she said with a mix of playfulness and concern. I hesitated to tell her what was on my mind; I couldn't bring myself to burden her with my worries.

"Just thinking about how lucky I am," I said with a forced smile that I hoped looked natural.

"Oh, is that so?" she teased.

"Yeah," I said, pulling her closer. Our foreheads almost touched, and for a moment, everything else fell away. "You're here, aren't you?"

Her laugh bubbled up, warm and genuine, and I held onto it like a lifeline. For now, the shadows could wait. This moment was hers, and I wouldn't let anything taint it—not the trading floor, not Brad's warning, not the weight of that small box waiting patiently in my coat. But even as I lay there, cocooned in the warmth of her presence, I couldn't shake the feeling that a storm was brewing just beyond the horizon.

Shannon leaned in and pressed her soft lips against mine, sending a surge of heat through me. It was the kind of kiss that steadied me, yet left my thoughts in disarray. When she pulled away, she sat up, her red hair cascaded over her bare chest as she reached for her clothes.

"I've got a hearing today," she said briskly as she slipped into her blouse. "It's a tough one. Custody case. The mom's fighting for her kids, but the father's lawyer is ruthless."

I propped myself up and watched her as she dressed. The way she moved with purpose, and the determination etched on her face, captivated me. She was unstoppable, a force of nature. And yet, guilt gnawed at me as I thought about how much she didn't know about my world, my struggles, my plans.

"You'll win," I said softly, but my voice lacked its usual confidence.

She paused, glancing at me in the mirror. "You think so?"

I nodded, though my mind was far from her case. Watching her focus on her work was one of the things I loved most about her, but my own turmoil was too loud to ignore. She turned and caught my eye, a small crease forming between her brows.

"Michael, are you okay? What's on your mind?"

Her question caught me off guard, and before I could stop myself, the words spilled out: "Marry me."

The room fell silent. Shannon froze, and her jaw dropped in disbelief.

"What?" she whispered, barely audible. Panic began to take over me as I ran a hand through my hair.

"I… uh. I had it planned. This isn't how I wanted to ask. I was going to make it special, with candles, dinner, the whole thing. I have a ring! I can get it—" I looked into her eyes, my chest tightened as my words failed to express my feelings. "I meant it, Shannon. I want to spend my life with you."

For a moment, her expression was unreadable, and I felt the crushing weight of uncertainty. But then her eyes filled with tears, and she started laughing, a bright, joy-filled sound that broke the tension. I let out a loud breath of relief and jumped out of the bed. I grabbed my coat and pulled out the velvet box. I was stark naked, the cold nipped at my exposed body as I went down on one knee.

"Are you serious?" her voice trembled.

"Dead serious." My heart pounded as I opened the box and revealed a gold diamond-encrusted ring. An heirloom from my mother and her mother. "Shannon Clarke, will you marry m—"

"Yes! Oh my God! Yes! Of course, I'll marry you!"

I laughed at her impatience and slipped the ring on her dainty finger. It was the perfect fit. Shannon reached for my bare chest to pull me up. As she kissed me fiercely her tears dampened my cheeks but I didn't mind.

"Yeah?" I wiped away a rogue tear before she could see it.

"Uhm… Hell yes!"

Relief and joy surged through me, washing away the heaviness I hadn't realized I'd been carrying. I held her tightly, her head tucked perfectly into the curve of my neck as if it had always belonged there. For the first time in ages, everything felt right.

"I love you, Shannon," I whispered.

She tilted her head up slightly and whispered back. "I love you too, Michael."

"So, when do you want to get married?"

She pulled back suddenly, just enough to meet my gaze, a mischievous glint sparked in her eyes as her lips curled into a smile.

"This weekend," she said.

The clearing office hummed with subdued activity, the steady rhythm of adding machines underscoring clipped conversations. I barely noticed any of it. My focus was locked on the report in my hands, the numbers glared at me like a warning light.

"Another good day, Mr. Russo," the clerk said with a polite smile that didn't quite reach her eyes.

"Thanks," I muttered, unfolding my card carefully. My stomach tightened as I scanned the figures. I knew I'd have to sit and cross-reference it and I already suspected something would be off again.

But what?

I slipped my trading card and personal logbook back into my jacket pocket. Every trade I executed was meticulously logged, down to the second. Cross-referencing these records with my end-of-day profit-and-loss statements, I began spotting subtle discrepancies like small mismatched prices or quantities that seemed innocuous but didn't add up. When I raised these concerns, the clearing firm dismissed them as human error. Yet, the irregularities formed a pattern, one too consistent to ignore, hinting at something deeper beneath the surface.

"We'll need evidence," Brad's voice echoed in my mind. He wasn't just stating the obvious; his words carried the weight of hard-learned experience. I remembered the conversation vividly and the way he leaned across the table with urgency.

"Without evidence, we don't have a leg to stand on," he'd said, his eyes locked onto mine. "Gut feelings won't cut it, Mike. They'll twist our words and turn the tables. We need to track every broker's actions. We have to build the case brick by brick, or we'll have nothing. And we need a team."

At the time, I'd brushed it off as paranoia, thinking my instincts and earnings were enough. But now, Brad's words felt almost prophetic. He was right. But this evidence, although helpful, was just not enough. We would have to dig deeper to overthrow the sleazy brokers in the Merc.

My gaze scanned the clearing office, the activity around me barely registered as my mind tried to understand the situation I was in. Finally, my eyes landed on Dave. He leaned against a desk and chatted casually with another big-shot power broker. His laugh rang out a little too loud, a bit too smooth, and it worked on my nerves. When our eyes met, I gave him a pointed nod. He excused himself from the conversation and ambled over, his smile effortless but his eyes calculated as he approached me. I would hate to doubt Dave as a broker because he taught me the ropes and pointed me in the right direction, but I couldn't trust anyone.

"Michael!" He slapped my shoulder with that practiced familiarity. It was the same greeting he gave everyone, like he'd known them for years, even though we both knew it wasn't true.

He should just stab me in the back, instead.

"Big congrats are in order, huh?" Dave's grin stretched wider, its perfection almost too deliberate—too calculated. "Shannon's a catch. You're a lucky man."

His voice carried an exaggerated warmth, as though he were trying to sell sincerity in bulk. But his words rang hollow, like lines recited from a script. I studied his face, searching for cracks beneath the polished veneer of friendliness. There was something deeper there, lurking just out of reach, like a shadow behind a curtain. I didn't return his grin.

"Thanks, Dave. I appreciate it," I replied flatly as my grip tightened on the report. "But I'm not here to talk about the wedding."

"Oh?" He raised an eyebrow, feigning interest. "What's up?"

"For the past month, I've noticed some questionable behavior amongst the brokers in the pit." Independent traders like myself are getting squeezed on our orders . Some of the brokers are seeing us stuck in a losing trade and instead of trading with us they turn to their bagman and give the order to them and then we have to pay a higher price to get out.

The room seemed to grow quieter as the weight of my words pressed against us both, but I held his gaze and refused to let him look away. Dave grew uneasy under my scrutiny. Sweat began to drip down his forehead as he adjusted his posture. His hands slipped casually into his pockets and he tilted his head slightly.

"Come on, Mike. You've been killing it lately. What's there to complain about?" he said softly as if I were a child he needed to placate. "You've got to trust the process. These things that you're seeing... it has a way of evening out."

I kept my voice steady but firm. "Dave. It's my money."

His expression flickered, a shadow of unease crossing his face. "Look, Mike, you've got to trust the process These things even out in the end, you should know that by now."

"I'm finding it hard to trust you, Dave."

"Mikey relax. Besides, you've got bigger fish to fry, like a wedding to plan. Focus on that."

"I'm not here for wedding advice. I want the truth."

His attempt at deflection was too obvious. I clenched my jaw, my patience had run thin with him and his lies. The silence stretched between us as I studied his face, looking for a crack in the façade. Dave shifted his weight and his posture subtly changed. His eyes flicked toward the room, as if making sure no one was listening, then he leaned in closer.

"The truth?" he repeated mockingly, almost as if the word itself were a joke. "The truth is, you're doing better than most, my friend. Why rock the boat when you're on your way up?"

I stepped toward him threateningly but he stood his ground. "You're hiding something. And I swear when I find out what it is, all hell will break loose." He straightened up until we were almost nose-to-nose. A grin began to slowly spread on his smug face.

"I see the floor's toughened you up a bit, huh Mikey? You're living the dream, now and you think you made it in life. And hey," he shoved a finger in my chest, "you did. You fucking did it. So stop digging up shite and be happy with the pretty little fucking life you got before it's all taken away because you can't keep your nose out of the wrong arses. Trust me, this is a small price to pay compared to the others."

They'll twist our words and turn the tables.

Dave's nostril flared as he stood inches away from me. It seemed like hours until he finally backed off. I was about to respond but he held his finger up to stop me.

"Look, you're a good kid, I'd hate to see you lose everything." The threat was evident. "How about as an apology, let me throw you and Shannon a wedding after-party. Drinks, music, the works. My treat. I want to prove to you that I'm your friend." He feigned a sincere look and I froze in disbelief.

The audacity of his offer after threatening me. I knew he was trying to distract me but I hesitated before answering him. This could work in our favor.

"Sure, Dave." I forced a smile. "Shannon would love that." He grinned and said his goodbyes. I watched him walk off and felt a knot tightening in the pit of my gut that had nothing to do with wedding jitters.

CHAPTER SEVEN

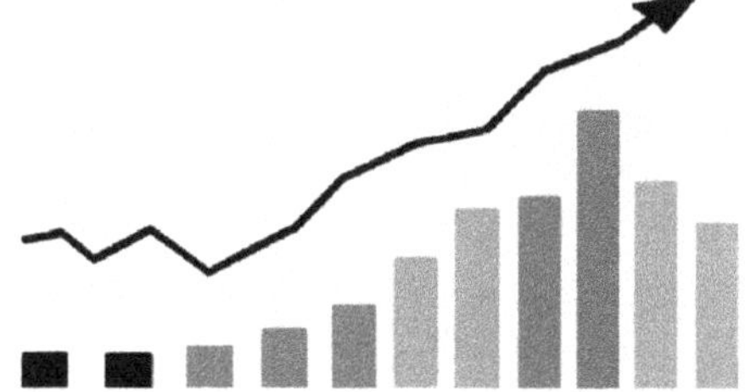

I adjusted my tie for what felt like the hundredth time. My reflection stared back at me, nervousness etched across my face. My fingers traced the fine threads of my suit as I tried to focus on steadying my breathing.

I'm getting married. Today. To Shannon. The woman who made everything in my chaotic world feel steady and real.

In the background, the sound of rowdy laughter erupted, causing my thoughts to scatter. Vince's booming voice carried over the noise. "Mike! You better not be chickening out, mate. Shannon's way out of your league as it is!"

"Don't listen to him," Steve chimed in, leaning against the doorframe with a beer in hand. "Shannon's settling. You've got that rugged charm, right? Or was it pity that won her over?"

Brad snorted from the corner, where he was lazily flipping through a newspaper. "You all shut the fuck up. Mike's already sweating through his suit, as is." I turned to look at them, a small smile broke through despite my nerves.

"You're all very comforting. Thanks for that," my tone dripped with sarcasm.

Owen whacked my back as he passed by, nearly making me stumble. "Come on, Mike, this is the biggest trade of your life. Just remember Shannon's the closing bell. Don't screw it up."

They all burst into laughter, the kind that reverberated through the room and somehow made the tension in my chest ease. These guys had seen me through some of the toughest days on the trading floor. Today, they were here to carry me through another big moment. I turned back to the mirror, straightening my jacket one last time.

This is it. My palms were clammy, and my gut twisted, but it wasn't fear. It was the weight of it all, the vows, the future, the unknown. And yet, beneath all of that, there was something stronger.

Shannon.

Her laugh, the way she tilted her head when she was teasing me, how her hand fit perfectly in mine. I pictured her walking down the aisle, and just like that, my nerves took a backseat.

"Mike!" Brad called, setting down his paper and walking over. He lowered his tone and all sense of the teasing was gone. "You've got this, man."

I swallowed hard. "Yeah. I do."

"Damn right, you do!" Vince added, clinking his bottle against Steve's.

The suit felt tighter than it had five minutes ago as Owen threw a casual comment my way. "So, Mike, you ready for that after-party Dave's setting up? Guy's pulling out all the stops for you." I tightened and loosened my tie, pausing to meet Owen's gaze in the mirror.

"No," I said bluntly. The room quieted. Vince raised an eyebrow, Steve stopped mid-sip of his beer, and Brad looked up from the corner.

"No?" Owen echoed curiously. I turned to face them, letting out a slow breath.

"Shannon and I decided to keep things small, just the ceremony, no big party. She's... not thrilled about Dave's offer, to be honest." The silence stretched, the room suddenly heavy with unspoken thoughts. Steve set his beer down on the counter with a soft thud.

"Shannon doesn't trust him either, huh?" he said quietly.

"She's not wrong," I admitted. My stomach twisted as I thought about my recent encounter with Dave and his awkward deflection and threats. The sick feeling in my gut hadn't left me since then.

"I ran into him recently. Same old Dave, acting like my best friend while dodging the questions that matter. Brad..." I glanced toward him, "You were right. Something is going on with the brokers. I see them clipping off the deck of the customers orders to offset any errors they have from the previous day. The ironic thing is that the exchange knows about this and condones this illegal behavior. It' despicable."

Brad stood abruptly, the chair creaked under him as he cut me off. "Not now, Mike."

"What do you mean, not now?" I snapped back. Built-up frustration bubbled to the surface. "You were the one who said we needed evidence and I'm trying to get that. I want to do something about it."

Brad crossed the room in two long strides, stopping just short of me. "And I stand by that," he said firmly. "But today isn't the day. Look around you. This is about you and Shannon. Not Dave and the Merc. You need to learn now that work stays at work. You never bring that shit into your home. Trust me."

Owen cleared his throat. "Brad's right," he said, stepping in to break the tension. "We can deal with Dave later. Today's about the good stuff." Steve and Vince mumbled in agreement.

"Yeah, man. Celebrate now; fight battles later. Let's not let that guy ruin the one day that's supposed to be perfect for you two." Steve offered a small comforting smile.

The anger simmered in my chest and cooled slightly, replaced by reluctant acceptance. Brad was right, again. Shannon deserved my full attention today, and I wasn't about to let Dave or anything else take that from her. I exhaled deeply, nodding.

"Sorry guys. We'll deal with this later."

Brad squeezed my shoulder, his grip was firm but reassuring. "Damn right, we will. Now let's get you married."

The others echoed their agreement and their laughter broke the tension as they returned to their usual antics. I adjusted my hair and struggled with my cuff links but eventually gave up on them and sat next to Steve who was red-faced from too much beer.

"Alright men, since you're all so full of wisdom today, how about some marital advice?" I asked and immediately regretted the question when Owen laughed.

"Don't look at me. I can't answer that! I'm single as ever, Mike. Ask me in ten years when I've maybe figured out dating."

"Noted," I said dryly. "How about you two? Don't look away!" I pointed at Steve and Vince as they purposefully tried to avoid the question.

"Well, shit!" Steve set his beer down with a dramatic sigh. "Marital advice? Easy. Don't upset her. Ever. If Cynthia's mad, I fear for my life. She once threw my golf clubs at me because I missed dinner. I swear one day that woman is going to kill me." The room erupted in laughter and Owen nearly fell out of his chair.

"Solid advice," I managed between chuckles. "Don't piss off your wife. Got it."

Vince grinned, joining in. "Here's a freebie, communication is key, but never underestimate the power of silence when you're wrong. You can't dig a hole if you don't start digging."

"Profound," I said, rolling my eyes. "Silent guilt over loud stupidity. I'll keep it in mind."

Brad leaned against the wall, arms crossed, a smirk playing on his face. "Here's mine," he said, his voice cut through the laughter. "Don't ever cheat. Two women? Twice the drama. Trust me, I've learned the hard way."

Owen shook his head, grinning. "Hard way or the stupid way?"

"Both," Brad admitted with a shrug, and even he couldn't suppress his laugh as the room dissolved into another round of jokes and jeers.

Before I could respond, the door creaked open and my dad stepped in, looking sharp in his suit but wearing that expression only a father could—a mix of pride and quiet authority.

"It's time, Michael," he said. His face was a kaleidoscope of emotions: pride, anxiety, and joy. "Now hurry up, or she'll think you bailed."

"You got this, soldier," Owen said.

I gave the guys a mock salute, Brad straightened my tie one last time, and I squared my shoulders.

"Let's get you married, son!" Brad bellowed as we marched out of the room.

I STOOD AT THE ALTAR WITH MY HANDS CLASPED IN FRONT OF ME. My heart thudded in time with the music and the doors opened slowly. Shannon stood at the entrance with her father. She looked stunning and I felt like the luckiest man on earth.

That's my bride.

All my nerves relaxed when she moved toward me with a grace that seemed effortless, her white dress caught the light just enough to make her glow. My chest tightened with pride and love. In a few minutes she was going to be my wife, and I couldn't hold back my smile and tears. When she finally stood before me and I saw her crying too, I longed to comfort her. A red curl escaped from beneath her veil and I admired how beautiful she looked.

In that moment, everything else faded—the noise, the nerves, and the room full of people. It was just us, and I knew, deep down, that we were starting something extraordinary. Her father handed her to me and I felt the warmth of her hand in mine as I watched as our fingers interlocked perfectly together.

Music, laughter, and endless energy filled the room as the after-party commenced. Shannon and I danced until our legs felt like jelly, her laughter mixed with the buzz of conversation and clinking glasses. The room spun with joy, faces blurred together in the dim light, and it was perfect chaos. When we finally sat down to catch our breath, the speeches resumed. The microphone passed from hand to hand, bringing warm toasts and a few roasts, each one met with cheers and laughter. Then Dave took the mic.

"Let me tell you about Michael," he began smoothly and confidently, like he was born to command attention. "When he first walked onto that trading floor, I wasn't sure he'd survive a week. But not only did he survive, he thrived."

The room clapped, but I barely heard it. My eyes flicked toward Vince, then Brad, and the knowing glances we exchanged were all too telling. Steve shifted in his seat, his expression tight and anxious, while Owen straightened up with a hard look on his face.

Dave continued, oblivious to their reaction and as if he were speaking to a crowd of traders on the floor. "Michael adapted faster than anyone I've ever seen," he said, reverently. "He's sharp, he's driven, and if today proves anything, it's that he's not just a great trader but a great man too. Truly, Mike, I'm proud of you."

Then, turning his attention to Shannon with a smile as smooth as his words, he added, "And Shannon, you've got yourself a man who doesn't just chase success but earns it. You two are a power couple in every sense. I can't wait to see where you'll go together."

The applause swelled as everyone cheered for us again. Dave was a questionable man but my focus was on Shannon. Her hand was warm on my arm, the ring on her finger shone brightly and her hair was undone from all the dancing. I looked at her face and was surprised to see her frowning.

"What's going on with you and your friends? And don't tell me it's nothing. I saw those looks." My chest tightened.

She didn't miss a thing.

"We'll talk about it later," I promised, brushing my thumb over her hand to calm her. "Right now, we have a honeymoon to think about. And tonight..." I spoke in what I thought was a seductive voice, "...I'm looking forward to spending the night with my wife." Her cheeks flushed a pretty pink, and she smiled, her curiosity momentarily replaced by something softer.

"You're a charmer, Mr. Russo," she murmured, shaking her head.

"That's why you married me, Mrs. Russo." I winked and she giggled.

The music pulsed as the wedding party raged on. The guests fully immersed themselves in the celebration. I was taking a breather by the edge of the room and scanning the scene with a mix of satisfaction and vigilance. Shannon danced with her sisters and relatives and the scene was one to remember, until I saw Dave at the corner of the grand hall. He handed something small and unmistakable to one of Shannon's cousins. I put down my drink and stalked toward him. My fists curled in anger as I pushed through the crowd until I reached him and pulled him aside.

"What the hell do you think you're doing?" I hissed.

Dave grinned, unbothered by my fury. "Relax, Mike. It's just a little fun. No harm, no foul."

"No harm?" I growled quietly so no one would hear us. Dave's cocky demeanor was pissing me off but I remained calm. "I don't want that shit anywhere near my family. Not here. Not tonight."

He looked infuriatingly smug. "C'mon, don't be such a boy scout. You're better than that." Before I could respond, Brad appeared, his face dark with anger.

"What's going on here, Mikey?" he growled.

"Brad, my man! I got a little something for you too," Dave said mockingly as he pulled out a little plastic bag filled with pills.

I barely had time to process what was happening when Brad shoved Dave with a force that sent him stumbling backward, his arms flailing to regain balance and the pills flew out of the packet and scattered around him. The sound of his body skidding across the asphalt echoed in the stillness of the night.

"Get the hell out," Brad growled, his stance wide and ready, shoulders tense, fists clenched at his sides. Dave, for a second, looked almost shocked, but that faded quickly, replaced by a twisted smirk.

"Touch me again, and I'll make you regret it," he sneered as he got up and dusted himself off.

Brad didn't flinch but stepped closer, closing the gap between them. "You've crossed the line, Dave."

With a sudden, swift movement, Dave threw a punch aimed at Brad's jaw but he dodged just in time, his reflexes fast. He missed the punch by inches, and Brad retaliated with a sharp shove to his chest, sending him stumbling backward once more.

"Fucking stop!" I yelled just as Owen, Vince, and Steve appeared. They looked at each of us completely bewildered.

"This is how you repay me?" Dave spat at me, straightening his jacket. "After everything I did for you?" Brad took a threatening step toward him again, his fists ready, but Owen grabbed him and held him back.

"*Everything you did*? You mean stealing from us and using it to play Mr. Big Shot? This whole damn party was funded with dirty money that belongs to us. Don't pretend you're the hero here, Dave," Brad spat at him.

Dave's cocky mask cracked just slightly, but he quickly recovered. "You're making a big mistake," he said, his voice low and venomous. "You'll regret this. All of you. "

Brad glared at him. "The only mistake was trusting you in the first place."

Dave flipped him the finger and walked off into the night, leaving a trail of tension in his wake. Brad turned to me, his jaw tight with anger.

"Sorry about that, Mikey. Let's get back inside. This night belongs to you and Shannon."

"It's alright," I said calmly, but for the rest of the night Dave's threats lingered darkly in the back of my mind.

7970

CHAPTER EIGHT

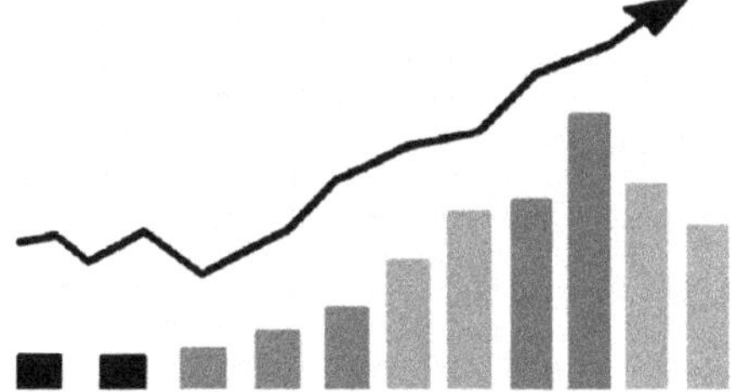

The cab ride from O'Hare to Brad's place in Lincoln Park felt like a sprint against time. Chicago's icy December air slapped me in the face the second I stepped outside, a stark contrast to the warm Hawaiian breeze I'd just left behind. I was late, but Shannon had insisted I make this meeting, no matter the jet lag.

Her words echoed in my mind: *"If you don't stand up now, then who will?"*

Brad's townhouse was nestled on a quiet street and the sound of muffled voices carried through the door before I even knocked. Brad himself opened it, his face lighting up the second he saw me.

"Russo! About time! How was Hawaii? Did you get lei'd or just laid?" He grinned, pulling me into a half-hug.

I smirked. "Both, if you must know. How's Chicago without me?"

"Colder. Literally and metaphorically," Brad quipped, leading me through a long passageway. His voice was light but with an edge of seriousness underneath. "I've gathered a little more men, Mike. The floor's been getting more tense with each passing day. The brokers are still confidently controlling things."

"We'll need all the firepower we can get," I replied.

Brad frowned in concentration. "It's tough, all the independent traders are scared of pissing off these brokers. We're going to need you and Owen to assist us with recruiting more of them. You guys are young, fiery, and climbing the ladder faster than us. They would respect you more."

I soaked in everything Brad said as we walked into his living room. There was a little chaos of folding chairs and chattering. I quickly counted seven traders, less than I'd expected. Vince and Steve sat near the window, gesturing animatedly as they argued over God knows what. A couple of heads turned to glance at me, one of them muttering something I couldn't catch.

"Man, you weren't kidding about them being scared," I said, scanning the room.

Brad swung his arm around my shoulder. "It's a big deal, Mike. People aren't ready to talk about it. Anyway, you missed the warm-up, but you're just in time for the fireworks."

Steve waved me over. He smelt like alcohol already and I couldn't help but chuckle at his predicament. "Hey, honeymoon boy! Did you bring me one of those floral shirts?"

"Sorry, Steve. I was too busy with my wife to think about you."

"That's my boy!" He grabbed my hand and shook it violently.

"Glad you're here, son. Owen couldn't make it. Said he had some big date." Vince added, looking too sober next to Steve.

"Classic Owen," I said, shaking my head. "So, what's the plan here?"

Before anyone could answer, a sharp voice cut through the room. "Can we trust him?"

The chatter stopped and all eyes turned to the speaker, a wiry man with slicked-back hair and features that reminded me of a rat who was pointing at me. I vaguely recognized him from the floor. His name escaped me but the hostility in his tone didn't.

"He's always up Dave's arse," he continued, jabbing a fat finger in my direction. "How do we know he's not just here to spy?"

A ripple of unease swept through the room. My jaw tightened, and I straightened up, meeting his glare head-on.

"If I were here to spy, I'd have better things to report than a room of just seven traders pissed off about dual trading," I said calmly.

Brad stepped in before things escalated. "Alright, Luke let's all calm down. Michael's one of us. He's seen the bullshit firsthand, just like the rest of you."

"Have I worked with Dave? Sure," I added, my tone sharper now. "But that doesn't mean I like what's going on. Ask anyone on the floor. It's not just shady, it's killing us—our clients and the Merc. You think I flew halfway around the world, fresh off my honeymoon, just to waste time here?"

Luke muttered curses under his breath. Before I could say anything, Brad clapped his hands together for our attention. "Now that we've cleared that shit up, let's get back to the real issue: How we're going to stop the bastards bleeding us dry."

Brad stood at the head of the room, flipping through a notepad as the rest of us gathered around. The air was thick with tension and cigarette smoke. I set my bag down and pulled out my statements, and trading cards; spreading them across the table like evidence in a courtroom. These records weren't just numbers; they were proof of what was happening on the floor.

Brad tapped his pen against his notepad to get everyone's attention. "Alright, listen up. We all know why we're here. Dual trading is killing the CME."

He paused as his gaze swept the room. "For those of you living under a rock, here's how it works: Brokers execute trades for their clients while also trading for their own accounts. In theory, it's fine. In practice, it's a disaster. Orders for their own accounts are prioritized, clients get screwed, and we're left to clean up the mess. Meanwhile, they're pocketing the difference."

The room murmured. Vince lit a cigarette, exhaling sharply. "And let's not forget the cherry on top: These guys flaunt their gains like they're untouchable. New Porsches, wild parties, and the abuse of drugs are growing rapidly on the floor."

Steve nodded, running a hand through his hair. "Yeah, the floor's turned into a circus. Everyone's either on something, flaunting something, or plotting to get ahead. It's not trading anymore. It's survival of the dirtiest."

Brad's voice was laced with frustration. "They're siphoning off the top, plain and simple. And we're supposed to just accept it."

An elderly trader I didn't recognize raised his hand. "I've seen it happen too. Orders 'accidentally' lost, trades reported at the wrong price, it's all part of the game. And the CME turns a blind eye because these guys bring in volume."

The conversation heated up as more men shared their experiences. Stories of brokers cutting corners, manipulating markets, and pressuring independents to stay silent poured out like a dam had broken. The anger was palpable as years of frustration bubbled to the surface.

Just as Brad was about to speak again, the door creaked open. Owen walked in, his shoulders slumped and a sour expression on his face.

"Let me guess," Vince said, smirking. "The date didn't go well."

Owen threw his hands up. "Don't get me started. She spent the whole night talking about her cat. And not in a cute way."

The room erupted in laughter, the tension momentarily broken. Even Brad cracked a smile before snapping back to business.

"Alright, take a seat Owen, and let's get back to the matter at hand," Brad said, his tone serious again. "We have two options: Keep our heads down and let this corruption keep bleeding us dry, or take a stand. But we need proof, and we need to stick together."

I leaned forward, my voice steady. "I've got the proof. But this isn't just about numbers. It's about taking back the floor. It's about trading fair and it's about us, working as a team."

Owen plopped into an empty chair, shaking his head. "Well, at least one of us had a productive night."

"Not really, we still don't have a plan on how to stop dual trading on a prominent exchange such as the Merc," I retorted.

Vince suddenly got up from his chair and adjusted his tie like he was in a courtroom. "Alright, let's think about this logically. The CME's not going to just upend their entire system because we're angry. We need a legal foothold. Dual trading is technically allowed under their rules, but there's a fine line when it comes to fraud. We need to document every instance where these brokers prioritize their accounts over clients'."

Brad crossed his arms. "Easier said than done, Vince. These guys cover their tracks well."

"That's why we focus on patterns," Vince replied, his tone measured. "We compile evidence showing the discrepancies between execution times, prices, and client losses. If we can prove a pattern of behavior, we might have a case for arbitration, or even take it to the SEC."

I thought of the conversations Shannon and I had on the beach in Hawaii. "Shannon mentioned something similar. She said we need to hit them where it hurts—their reputation. If we bring this to light, the CME will have no choice but to act. They're not going to risk public backlash."

Vince pointed at me. "Exactly. And while arbitration is a good start, public pressure could be our best weapon. Think about it, if the press gets wind of traders being cheated while the exchange turns a blind eye, they'll have to clamp down."

Steve frowned, a fresh glass of whiskey in his hand. "But what if they come after us instead? These guys have deep pockets and connections

"That's why we stick to facts," Vince said firmly. "No accusations we can't back up."

"Then every discrepancy must be supported by hard evidence." Steve looked at the men seated in the room with a determination I'd never seen before.

Although I only saw Vince and Steve under celebratory circumstances, I knew they were well-respected traders on the floor. And seeing them take charge as leaders was inspiring. Owen and I agreed to stick by them when they entered the scene—we learned a lot from their experience, and now we were going to learn how to overthrow the thieving brokers.

I gestured to my stack of paperwork again. "I got that covered, Steve, but we're going to need more men on the job.

Brad nodded slowly. "Alright. So, we gather evidence, build a timeline, and present it to the CME. But what if the bastards still don't budge?"

"Then we go public," Vince said simply. "The Chicago Tribune loves a good scandal. 'Independent Traders Stand Against Corruption'—that kind of headline will make waves."

The room buzzed with cautious agreement. A few traders muttered about their own experiences, and one guy slammed his fist on the table.

"I'm in," he said gruffly. "These bastards have screwed me over for the last time."

As the plan started to take shape, Brad turned to me and Owen. "You're on board with this?"

I met his gaze. "One hundred percent. This isn't just about us, it's about fixing the floor and saving the customers. I'm tired of playing by the rules that only work for them."

"I agree, this is our money on the line too," Owen said.

Vince rubbed his hands together. "Then it's settled. We start with documentation and gaining more men on our team."

The room buzzed with resolve, but I couldn't shake the feeling of uncertainty. We were going up against powerful brokers, like Dave. I shivered at the memory of his threats, although nothing had happened to me, Owen, or Brad yet. I looked around at the faces of the other traders and felt a spark of hope.

At least we're not alone in this.

I packed up my notes while the room hummed with half-hearted conversations. Most of the guys were starting to filter out, leaving only the faint smell of whiskey and cigars lingering in the air. Steve, clearly buzzed, leaned over to Vince, flashing that typical playful grin of his.

"I forgot you actually studied law, Vince. You're such a dumb-fuck most of the time," Steve joked, slurring slightly as he swayed on his feet.

Vince, without even lifting his eyes from my notes, shot back dryly, "How many drinks have you had, Steve?"

Brad chuckled, eyeing Steve with a mix of amusement and exasperation until he saw the empty bottle on the floor.

"What the fuck, Steve? You drank my expensive whiskey. This isn't a fucking party."

Steve laughed heartily and we couldn't help but join in, shaking our heads at his antics. I looked over at him, his face flushed with alcohol, and sighed. I shoved my papers into my bag and stood up, already feeling the weight of the night lifting.

"I'll take Steve home," I said as I followed him to the door.

He swayed and walked, clearly a little too deep in his cups, but I figured I'd get him to his place without much trouble. We said our goodbyes and left. The drive to his house was quick, just a few roads away from Brad's, and I was eager to get him out of there before he could get into any more trouble. As we stumbled through Steve's doorway, Cynthia's voice rang out from the hallway, sharp and teasing.

"You better not be drunk, Steve!" He looked completely unfazed and waved her off like it was no big deal.

"Yeah, yeah, I'm not," he said, barely pausing as he passed by her.

Cynthia reached out and smacked him lightly on the back of the head, her lips pursed and nose crinkled as she smelt the alcohol on her husband. Steve fell on the floor feigning a serious injury from his wife's light smack and she struggled not to laugh. She glanced up at me with a tight smile while Steve rolled around the carpeted floor. It was a scene to remember.

"Thank you, Michael," she said softly. "The wedding was lovely. And I'm so sorry about this man-child." I stood by the front door, watching as Steve struggled to stay steady. I struggled to suppress a laugh. Cynthia shot him an exasperated look but didn't say anything as she turned to me.

"Thanks for getting him home."

"It's no problem at all, Cynthia. You take care now," I replied, nodding toward her before turning back to Steve who shot me a thumbs-up as the door closed.

As I headed to my car, a chuckle escaped me from thinking about my friends' antics. The chaos of the night had finally settled, and my thoughts turned to the bonds we'd forged. Brad, Vince, Steve, and Owen weren't just colleagues; they were family. These were the people who stood by me through every storm. For them, I'd go to the ends of the earth. No matter the stakes, even if my own life were on the line, I'd fight for them without hesitation.

CHAPTER NINE

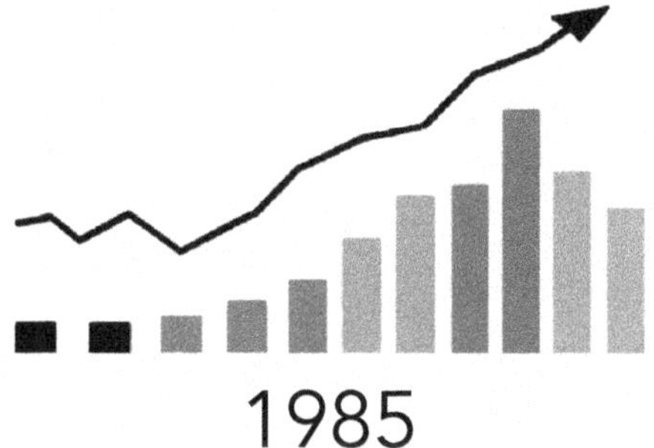

1985

The floor bustled with its usual frenzy, a mixture of shouts and hand signals that somehow made perfect sense to those who thrived in it. Owen and I, dressed in our unmistakable neon-yellow jackets, stood out not just for our colors but for what they represented: precision, confidence, and the respect of nearly everyone in the pits. Life felt like a series of highs, and the money flowed as fast as the trades we executed. But behind the rush of it all, a gnawing unease persisted. Dual trading was rife, and the lifestyle in the Merc was changing drastically. Owen elbowed me, pulling my focus from the big board.

"Look at that." He gestured toward the far end of the floor. Ronnie Weinberg slipped through the crowd, his steps quick and purposeful as he ducked into the bathroom. "There he goes again. What do you think? His daily dose of adrenaline?"

I snorted and leaned closer. "Adrenaline on the floor's not enough for some people, huh?"

"Guess not. Maybe I should start disappearing mid-shift too. Keep everyone guessing."

"Sure," I said, raising an eyebrow. "Until you miss a trade and spiral."

"Hey," Owen shot back with a grin. "You're not wrong. I'd lose my damn mind."

I laughed, shaking my head, but my gaze lingered on the bathroom door. Ronnie wasn't the only one chasing a different kind of high. Some guys needed the rush of the floor to spill over. The booze, the powder, the recklessness, it was all out in the open—just enough to see but not enough to challenge. Everyone looked the other way and ignored the impending doom.

"Think he'll ever slow down?" Owen asked, his voice quieter now.

"Ronnie?" I shook my head. "Doubt it. Guys like that are addicted to more than the rush of the floor."

Owen gave a low whistle, leaning back against the wall. "Not sure whether to envy him or feel sorry for him."

I glanced at Owen. "Don't envy him, that's for sure. Not everyone who burns hot sticks around long." He gave a short nod before returning his focus to the pit, gesturing wildly at a clerk as he shouted an order. The energy of the place was magnetic, a pull that was hard to resist.

But I couldn't help one thought from creeping in: *at what cost?*

Apart from Ronnie's predictable bathroom trips, I started noticing other guys discreetly popping pills or ducking into corners to snort a quick line. Their actions were subtle, but the aftermath was obvious. Eyes wide and too focused, sweat dripping down their brows despite the winter chill outside. It wasn't adrenaline. It was something far heavier, far riskier. I watched one trader stumble as he tried to bark out an order, his voice cracked mid-yell. His hands trembled as he made a signal, his clerk looking more concerned than confused. This wasn't the sharp, precise intensity of the pits—it was disgraceful.

Owen nudged me again, his voice low. "You see that? Ben over there. He's been tweaking all week."

I followed his gaze through the crowd. "Yeah, I see it. It's getting worse."

"You think they'll do something about it?" he asked, but his tone was already resigned.

I shook my head, letting out a slow breath through my teeth. "As long as the trades keep flowing, no one's gonna care. But it's starting to spill over."

Owen leaned closer, his voice low enough to cut through the noise without being overheard. "You know what this means, don't you?" He motioned with a nod toward Benny, who was wiping sweat off his face with a trembling hand. "It's not just them screwing up their trades. It's the clients, the clerks, the whole damn system. One guy blows a deal because he's too strung out, and we all feel it."

I nodded, my eyes narrowed in Benny's direction. "I've seen it. Sloppy hand signals, bad calls. The ripple effects are everywhere."

"This place is like a ticking time bomb," Owen muttered. "One of these guys is gonna spiral out, and we'll all pay for it."

"Yeah," I replied. "And Management's got their heads so far up their asses counting profits they'd rather risk a blowup than address the mess."

Owen's expression was grim. "You're okay with that? Just letting them drag us down with them?"

"Of course I'm not okay with it," I shot back, the frustration leaking into my voice. "But what do you want me to do? Stand on a chair and yell, 'Hey, keep your coke binges at home?' These guys aren't listening to anyone, especially not us."

A bitter laugh escaped his lips. "It's funny, isn't it? We're supposed to be the sharpest guys in the room, the ones running this circus. And yet, we're watching it all burn."

I sighed and glanced at the bathroom where Ronnie had disappeared. "I'm not against what they do on their own time, Owen. Hell, I've had my fun too. But the floor? This isn't the place."

"Yeah, well, tell that to Ronnie and the rest of them. The drugs are going to kill them one of these days. I just hope it won't be in the pit." I grimaced at his words. "And that's what scares me the most."

"Keep it out of work," I muttered, more to myself than to Owen. "If they can't even manage that then what the hell are we doing here?"

Owen raised an eyebrow. "You gonna say something?"

"To who?" I asked bitterly. "The same guys who are raking in the cash for drugs and dual trading? They'll laugh me off the floor."

His lips pressed into a thin line. "Guess it's just another thing we have to work around, huh?"

I didn't answer, but my mind churned as I glanced at the men shouting, laughing, and sweating in their frenzied haze. I couldn't help but wonder how much longer we could hold it all together before the world found out the truth about the CME's lifestyle.

Vince muttered, crossing his arms. "They're hedging on their own trades using our backs as leverage." The independent traders are getting less and less trades and all the trades are going to the bagmen and then back to the brokers.

Steve let out a sharp laugh. "What do we do? Storm the goddamn pits? Light their jackets on fire?"

Brad whipped around, pointing a finger at him. "You think this is funny, Steve? They're fucking bleeding us dry, and you're cracking jokes. Grow the fuck up."

Steve shrugged, smirking. "What the hell do you want me to do, Brad? Cry about it?"

"Shut up, both of you," I cut in, slamming my logbook shut. "This isn't helping. We're not going to win by yelling at each other."

Brad scowled, rubbing his temples. "Win? We're not winning shit, Michael. We don't have enough proof, or men, and not a single person in this godforsaken building gives a damn."

Owen nudged the papers closer, his tone quieter but no less bitter. "We can't even get half the floor to back us. Everyone's either too scared or too busy licking the brokers' boots."

I exhaled in frustration. "Numbers alone aren't enough. We need something solid—, anything to make this undeniable."

"And what then?" Vince asked. "You think the Exchange will suddenly grow a conscience? You think anyone up there gives a shit about us?"

The silence hung heavy, the weight of his words sinking in. Deep down, we all knew the answer.

Brad finally spoke, his voice low and rough. "They don't care. And they never will. We're just bodies to them, expendable."

Owen sighed, running a hand through his hair. "This fight feels like punching a brick wall. We're wasting time."

I stared at the trading cards again, the jagged numbers mocking me. It wasn't just the money. It was the principle, the way they thought they could screw us over without consequence. But staring at the defeated faces of my friends, a bitter thought crept in.

Maybe they were right and this fight was already lost. Before I could fully sink into the thought, a voice broke through the tense silence.

"I can't get out of any trades?" A young trader, fresh to the floor and still trying to find his footing, stood at the center of the clearing office, his face etched with frustration. He was still new, a little rough around the edges, but the anger in his eyes was clear. He waved his trading cards in the air.

His hands shook slightly as he clutched his trading card, and his face flushed with panic and outrage. He wasn't used to being ignored. This was about trust, and right now, it felt like everything he'd worked for had been stolen from him.

I know the feeling all too well.

He yelled at one of the clerks, and the tension in the room immediately spiked.

"What the hell is this, huh? Are you people fucking me over? And don't lie to me! Your fucking brokers are being selective too!" He waved his fist in the clerk's face.

The room shifted uncomfortably and a couple of brokers rushed over, trying to calm him down, but the young guy wasn't having it.

"Speak of the fucking devils!"

"Calm down, young man." One of the brokers said confidently.

"Don't tell me to calm down, you prick!" he snapped back. "I'm tired of this bullshit!" The tension in the room escalated as his words bounced off the walls. No one was used to seeing this kind of scene from someone this new.

I exchanged a quick look with Owen and I could see the wheels turning in his head.

"You wanna intervene? This could be our chance to gain more men in our team." I whispered.

Owen's face hardened at the implication of my question. "There's no going back if we do."

We both understood but we couldn't just stand there and let the opportunity go to waste. A beat of silence passed, and without another word, we both started moving toward the young trader. I could feel the heat of the tension with every step.

"Hey, hey, calm down," I said, holding my hands up as we approached.

The young guy's eyes were wide with anger, as he whirled around. "Calm down? You think I'm gonna just sit here while you guys steal trades from me?"

I took a breath. "We understand but you've got to take a step back."

He paced back and forth, the anger in his voice growing. "I worked on Wall Street before this. I know how it's supposed to work. But here? Something's wrong, and I'm going to figure it out."

Owen stepped in, his tone a little firmer. "If you want to do something about it then I suggest you shut the fuck up and come see us outside."

The young trader stalked forward, his fists clenching. "You're full of shit. I'm done playing games with big shots like you." His voice rose.

I grabbed his wrist gently but firmly. "Listen, kid. We know things aren't perfect. But you have to stay cool."

But that only made him snap. He jerked his arm away from me. "Cool? I've been cool long enough!"

He was shaking, his face flushed. The broker who had tried to calm him earlier stepped forward again, his voice desperate. "We'll get it worked out. Just take a breath. Don't escalate it."

The room grew quieter as more traders started paying attention, and the murmurs turned into whispers. Some of them looked nervous. Others were just waiting for the storm to pass.

Then, with a sudden snap of his head, the young man shouted, "You think I'm going to just keep quiet while you fat cats get paid for my hard work?"

I leaned closer to the boy, my voice low but calm. "This isn't the way to fix it, trust me."

"I've been here six months, busting my ass, and they're fucking me over! I just know something ain't right!"

I glanced over at Owen. "We've got to get him to chill before this gets any worse."

Owen looked back at me steadily. "We don't have time for this bullshit. Let's wrap it up."

At that moment, a chorus began, murmurs of agreement from other traders. The chaos was about to explode, and we needed to act fast.

"Hold on," someone from the crowd shouted, eyes narrowing at the broker. "Are you telling us that our money from the trades is being stolen? You'd better explain yourself, because we're not just going to stand here and take it!"

The broker, suddenly on the defensive, shifted uncomfortably under the collective gaze. Other traders started chiming in. Some of them angry, others confused, their voices rising in a crescendo.

“Is this happening to all of us?” one of them barked, his eyes wild. “What the fuck is going on here?”

The panic spread like wildfire, and I saw a few men glance nervously at each other. Traders who usually shouted across the pits without a second thought now looked rattled. They hadn’t seen anything like this before. Brad stepped forward, his eyes blazing with frustration. I was surprised he stayed silent that long.

“Shut the hell up, all of you!” he roared over the noise. Everyone froze, their eyes locked onto him. The room was dead silent for a moment, the air thickened with unease.

“Stop standing around and complaining like a bunch of pussies!” Brad barked, his face red with anger. “If you want to fix this shit, we do it together. So if you want to do something about it like real men then come see us outside, and we’ll give you the truth. But if you just want to stand there, bitching and moaning, nothing will change.”

The atmosphere was heavy with frustration. Some of the traders were nervous, others desperate for answers, but most of them simmered with anger. One thing was clear, they were ready to listen and they were ready to act.

“Who do we talk to then?” The young trader asked, his anger suppressed as he looked at Brad for answers.

“If you fucking listened in the first place you would’ve known who was willing to help you.” Brad gestured with a nod towards me and Owen.

The traders looked at us confused and concerned. I cleared my throat.

“Meet us outside,” I said to them.

CHAPTER TEN

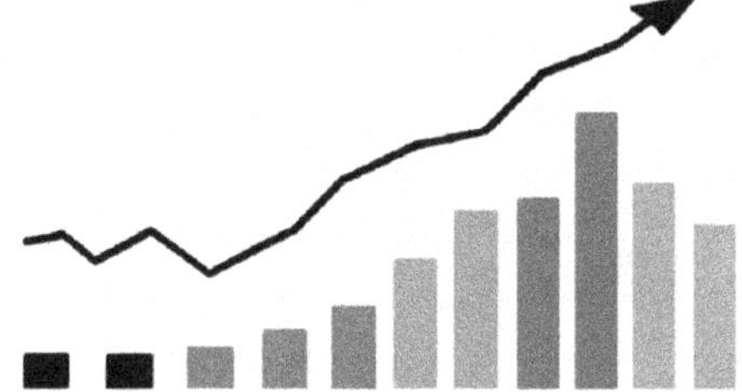

In the weeks that followed the tension on the trading floor was palpable. Traders spilled into conversations and quiet complaints. They were fed up with the underhanded manipulation by the power brokers. Owen and I kept our ears open and watched tempers flare like gas-fed flames. It all came to a head during a hastily arranged meeting in the breakroom. The air was thick with the acrid smell of burnt coffee, and the room buzzed with a mix of anger and desperation.

"This is bullshit!" The young trader from the clearing room incident—whose name was Jerry—spat, his face red with anger and frustration. "We bust our asses on the floor and they're sitting pretty, skimming off the top!"

Owen nodded toward me, signaling for support. I stepped forward. "We all see it, Jerry, but yelling about it doesn't change anything. We need a plan, not just outrage."

Brad, ever the loose cannon, took center stage. He slammed his fist on the table, rattling the Styrofoam cups. "You're damn right we need a plan. But first, grow some balls, all of you!" His voice boomed over the murmurs. "They're fucking us over, and we just bend over and take it? Not me. Not anymore."

The room fell silent. Even the naysayers seemed shaken by his conviction.

Owen leaned toward me. "Brad's got the fire, but it won't mean shit without follow-through."

I nodded. "Let's harness it, then."

The next step was tricky. Pulling independent traders into an alliance meant navigating fear, distrust, and the overwhelming power of the brokers. Owen and I started small, holding quiet meetings after hours in the corner of an old diner near the Loop because it wasn't safe to bring this into our homes.

"We're not asking you to be heroes," I began during one of these meetings, my tone calm but firm. "We just want the truth to come out. Together, we have a chance."

A trader named Manny shook his head in fear. "You think the brokers will just roll over? They'll ruin us, Mike. Our reputations, our livelihoods, everything."

Owen stepped forward. "You really think this isn't happening already? We're scraping by while they sit back and pocket the difference. Brokers hold orders, direct them to theirbagmen, and we get the scraps. If the customers find out, it could blow up in all of our faces. This isn't just unfair, it's a racket." His words landed heavily on them, leaving the men silent as the reality of the situation began to sink in.

Our jobs were on the line.

"What would happen if the customers found out?" Jerry asked quietly.

Owen and the team looked at me for an answer. I leaned against the table, looking out at the room full of tense, expectant faces.

"Alright, good question Jerry. Let's talk about what happens if the clients find out about dual trading," I began with a firm and steady voice. "First off, they'll lose trust in the entire system. Once they see brokers manipulating their trades for profit, they'll start questioning the integrity of the markets altogether. And when trust goes? They pull their money."

I scanned the room, letting the weight of my words settle in. "Withdrawals won't be just a few accounts, it'll be a goddamn stampede. They'll go looking for firms they think are cleaner and safer. And it won't stop there. Clients that are pissed off enough could start filing lawsuits, alleging fraud, and they can demand their money back. Think of the chaos that would unleash not just in the CME but in our own personal lives as well."

I paused for effect and watched a few heads nod grimly. "Regulators like the CFTC? They'll come down hard. Investigations, fines, and maybe even bans for some of these firms. And while they're busy doing that, the confidence in the trading floor—what keeps this place alive—will go straight to hell. Markets thrive on trust, and if that goes, so does the stability."

Owen, standing next to me, folded his arms and added, "And don't think for a second they'll stop at the guilty. They'll torch everyone here just to make a point."

I met each trader's eyes. "So, yeah, the fallout would be brutal. But maybe that's exactly what's needed to clean up this mess."

"How can we help?" someone shouted from the back of the room.

I paused for a moment, gathering my thoughts. "We've been keeping detailed records of everything. Documenting every order, every discrepancy. But we know that won't be enough. So, our next step is to take this to the CME directly. We can't fight this alone anymore." The situation pressed down on all of us. We were about to go to war with the system itself.

I wished we had more leverage, something decisive that could force change, but the reality was stark: our best shot lay in strength in numbers. We needed more traders willing to risk their necks alongside us. Only then could we approach the CME, present a united front, and demand action. It felt like a gamble, relying on others to step forward in a cutthroat environment like this, but without them, our efforts would falter before they even got off the ground. The stakes were too high to go at it alone.

A floor manager of one the big brokerage houses spoke up. "I've been keeping detailed logs of every trade—times, prices, everything. I know they've been holding my orders and filling them at worse prices. The delays are obvious and the customers are fed up with bad fills on their orders. They're shortchanging us, no doubt about it."

Brad slapped his skinny shoulder. "That's the type of documenting we need. Now, imagine twenty or more of us approaching the CME with that kind of similar evidence. They'll have no choice but to acknowledge us."

The scrawny man nodded, but not everyone was convinced. Doubts lingered, especially among the older traders. The fear of losing it all held them back like chains.

As the group broke up that night, Owen muttered, "We've got a long road ahead."

I stared at the diner's flickering neon sign. "Yeah. But we're on it now, and there's no turning back."

The floor was chaos incarnate on a good day, but that day, something was off. I was mid-trade when a sharp voice broke through the noise.

"You think you're better than me, huh? Just because you're part of the old boys' club?" Jackson, an African-American trader, stood rigid, pointing at Thomas, a burly white veteran of the floor. This wasn't just a typical argument. They were both part of our meetings, and I had never seen them like this before.

"Old boys' club?" Thomas spat. "You're damn right I've been here longer. Maybe if you spent less time whining and more time learning, you'd get somewhere too!"

"Whining?" Jackson's voice cracked with anger. "And what should I learn? How to cheat and steal from other traders?"

"You're out of your mind," Thomas growled back. "You think you're entitled to anything just because you showed up? There's no way I can steal, I'm in the same boat as you!"

The surrounding noise died down. Traders stopped in their tracks, sensing the fight brewing. I moved forward, trying to intervene.

"Enough!" I said, holding up my hands. My voice sliced through the air, commanding attention.

Jackson shot me a glare. "What, Michael? You gonna tell me I'm wrong too?"

I took a deep breath, trying to stay calm. "This isn't the way, Jackson. And Thomas, back off. Both of you, get your heads out of your asses." They sneered at each other but didn't move.

"You gonna defend him? He's making accusations he can't back up!" Thomas shouted.

"And you're proving his point by acting like this," I shot back.

"How do I know you white folks are not in on this together?" Jackson's voice was tight with anger.

I looked at both of them, "This is exactly what the system is built on, divide and conquer. They keep us at each other's throats so we don't see what's really going on. Right now, you two are doing their job for them. This isn't a fight against the color of your skin. This is a fight against us, independent traders."

They held their breath. Jackson's hand twitched as if he was still considering throwing a punch and Thomas scowled but stayed quiet.

"Listen to me," I continued, my voice low but firm. "The real fight isn't with each other. It's with the brokers skimming off the orders. You're both angry, and you should be, but direct it where it belongs."

A heavy silence hung between us. Slowly, they stepped away from each other. I eyed them wearily before I weaved my way back to my usual spot. As the buzz of the floor resumed, Owen leaned toward me.

"You think that did anything?"

"Hopefully," I muttered, still watching Jackson and Thomas. "But this isn't the last of it. Those guys always got along, I wonder what's changed."

"Maybe it's an attack from the inside?" Owen was staring at the screens as he said this and something about the question made me feel uneasy.

Later that night, we all crammed into the Loop. The usual atmosphere of the bar changed into a war room. Our table was buried under trading cards,statements records, and handwritten notes. The air was thick with unease as the weight of what we were doing pressed down on all of us.

Owen leaned over the mess, tapping a folder. "This is it," he said, his voice low but charged. "I think we've got enough to make them sweat."

"Yeah, if we can keep it from blowing up in our faces," Vince muttered. He glanced around the room like he expected someone to bolt.

"What do you mean?" I asked, my stomach twisted into knots.

Vince sighed and rubbed his temples. "Someone's been talking. They know we're sniffing around."

Brad slammed a folder onto the table, making everyone flinch. " I lost over $100,000 today because I couldn't get out of a trade. Got pissed off and continued to fight the market until I was buried.

"I can't afford this," one guy said, his voice cracking. "I've got kids at home, a mortgage. If they pull something on me—"

"They won't stop with you," Brad cut in, his eyes blazing. "You think keeping your head down will save you? You're dreaming. If we don't stand up now, they'll bleed every one of us dry eventually. This isn't just about money, it's about showing them they can't keep screwing us over."

Owen nodded, his face set. "Brad's right. This is dangerous, we all knew that going in, but we're too far in to back out. The evidence we have can blow the lid off their whole operation, but only if we hold the line."

I stood, letting my gaze sweep the room. "Look, I get it. You're scared—I am too. But that fear? It means we're doing something they don't want us to. That's power. We've got them rattled. But this only works if we keep our heads. Tighten the circle. Watch what we say. And for God's sake, no more slip-ups." I turned toward Jackson and Thomas pointedly.

The room fell silent. I could feel the hesitation, the doubts circling like vultures. But no one moved. No one spoke up to back out.

Owen crossed his arms, his jaw tight. "This is it, folks. We're on the edge of something big. But it's now or never. You in or out?"

After a long, tense pause, Vince sighed. "In," he said, barely above a whisper.

One by one, the others echoed him.

Brad clapped his hands together, his grin grim. "Then let's show them what happens when you mess with the wrong people."

The pressure was suffocating, but we were locked in now. I stood at the front of the table, my gaze swept across the faces before me. The weight of the moment pressed on my chest. The evidence we'd collected was almost ready. But I knew that there would be consequences. Everything came at a cost.

"We can't back down now," my voice rang with urgency. "We're not just fighting the brokers. We're fighting the system itself. If we don't stand together, we'll lose. There's no middle ground here. We win or we lose as a group."

Owen stood beside me and didn't break eye contact with anyone. His jaw was tight, his expression grim. "If we pull back now, all of this, everything we've worked for, it's meaningless. We can't let them win. We have to push forward." I looked around and saw the fear and resolve.

"Tomorrow, we're taking a stand. It's bigger than us. Bigger than our careers. We're fighting for what's right. For everyone who's been hurt by this rigged system. But we can't do this alone. We have to stay united. We can't expose this just by talking or sending out a petition. We need solid proof of every instance of brokers holding orders, front running, and manipulating the market. We need to document everything, get sworn affidavits, and find witnesses. We'll create a case so airtight, they won't be able to ignore it."

Owen spoke up, his voice full of the same urgency I felt. "This isn't just about us on the floor. It's about the customers who never knew they were getting cheated. If we don't hit them where it hurts, legally and publicly, then nothing will change. And if the CME doesn't do anything about it then we got to go to the media and make it impossible to sweep under the rug."

Brad rose from his seat confidently. "We need to get the regulators involved. CFTC and SEC, whatever it takes. We've got to put the pressure on and make sure this doesn't get buried. But we have to be ready for retaliation. They already began."

"Exactly," I said, locking eyes with each of them. "If nothing is done once we file a complaint then we go public. We're going to need every single one of you, no one gets to back out now. We expose this, together." The room was silent for a moment as each man absorbed the enormity of what we were about to do.

Brad slammed his fist onto the table, his eyes blazing. "Let's fucking get it done, then."

And just like that, the decision was made. Tomorrow, we'd walk into the CME, armed with everything we'd gathered, ready to confront them about dual trading. We couldn't afford to back down now. We dove back into the evidence and worked well into the night, cross-referencing every incident and double-checking every claim. The hours blurred together, but each minute was critical. We were so close to exposing them, but we knew the risks. We could lose everything, our jobs, our finances, maybe even our lives.

CHAPTER ELEVEN

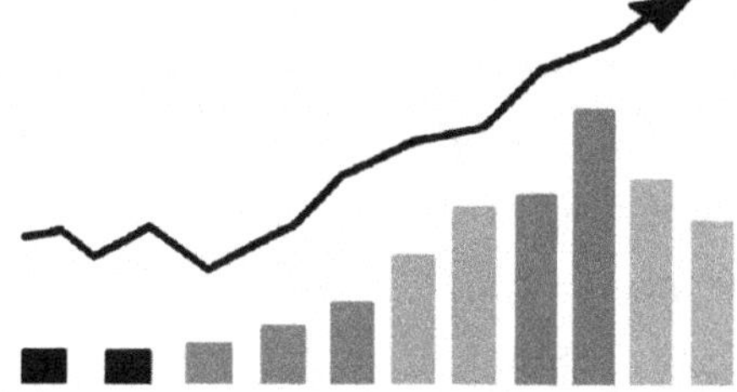

By morning, I had a stack of papers so neat it felt like a weapon in my hands. When I stepped into the CME building, the air felt heavier, like even the walls were judging me for what I was about to do. My shoes echoed against the marble floors, each step rang out like a warning, but I pushed forward.

At the reception desk, a woman glanced up, her expression teetering on unimpressed. "Can I help you?"

"Michael Russo. I'm here to file a formal complaint," I said, steady but clipped. "Compliance Department."

Her gaze flicked up to meet mine, a little more curious now, but she didn't ask any questions. Instead, she gestured to the left. "End of the hall. Room 312."

"Thanks."

I adjusted the folder under my arm and turned toward the hall she'd pointed to, my footsteps quieter now on the carpet. A small brass plaque on the door read *Compliance Department.* I knocked once.

"Come in."

The voice was low and serious, just enough to make me straighten up before turning the knob. Inside, the office was small, with no windows and barely enough space for the desk and two chairs. The man behind the desk stood when I entered. He looked like every middle manager you've ever seen: gray suit, thin tie, thinning hair. His eyes were sharp though, the kind that could pick apart a sentence before it finished leaving your mouth.

"You're Mr. Russo?" he asked, his voice measured.

"That's right," I said, closing the door behind me.

"It's nice to finally put a face to the name on everyone's lips. I've heard a lot about you. Have a seat."

"Thank you, Mr. Reynolds." He shook my hand firmly.

As I sat down I placed the folder carefully on the edge of his desk, like it might explode if I dropped it too hard. He eyed it for a moment, then looked back at me.

"And what exactly are you here for today?"

"To file a formal complaint," I said, steadily. "Against brokers on the S&P floor. Regarding the practice of dual trading which results in held orders, paying bagmen to cover losses, you name it. I've got evidence."

That got his attention. He leaned back slightly, but his expression didn't give much away. "Evidence?"

I pushed the folder toward him. "Every instance of broker misconduct over the last 6 months which were identified by a group of independent traders, this includes the bagmen they are partnering with to fraudulently use customer orders to benefit their personal accounts.

He opened the folder and flipped through the pages, his face unreadable. After a moment, he looked up at me. "You're claiming this is intentional? Deliberate misconduct?"

"Yes," I said, leaning forward. "And not just against me. This affects every trader on that floor. These brokers are holding orders to benefit their bagmen, guys like Seth Kaufman. It's all in there, clear as day if you know what you're looking at."

He didn't answer right away as his eyes scanned the documents again. Then he closed the folder and set it on the desk.

"We take these matters very seriously, Mr. Russo," his voice was clipped. "The evidence will be reviewed thoroughly, and appropriate action will be taken if misconduct is found."

"If?" I echoed, my frustration seeping through. "Everything you need is in that folder. What more do you need to see?"

"We'll review it," he repeated dismissively.

I stared at him, willing him to give me something, *anything*, that didn't sound like a brush-off. But he didn't. He just sat, calm and impassive, like this was routine for him. Eventually, I stood up, defeated.

"This isn't just about me, you know. This is about everyone who's getting screwed over by a system they can't fight."

He met my gaze but it didn't feel like he was really *hearing* me. "We'll be in touch, Mr. Russo."

I fought back the urge to argue. I wanted him to swear they'd act, to promise that justice would come swiftly, but all I got was bland, infuriating responses.

"Just... don't let this disappear."

Reynolds didn't say anything as I turned and walked out, but I could feel his eyes on my back. I stepped into the hallway, my pulse pounded in my ears. The walk felt longer on the way out.

This could be it. This could change everything.

But even as I walked, a small voice in the back of my head whispered something I didn't want to hear: *What if it doesn't?*

For the first time in weeks, I felt a sliver of hope as whispers traveled faster than any trade. It didn't take long for news to leak that power brokers had been called into the CME's offices. Word spread in waves, each retelling louder than the last.

"Did you hear? They hauled in Lawrence and Gadsen. Seth too."

"About time someone put a spotlight on them."

I tried to stay focused on my own trades, but I couldn't stop glancing at the clock. Every tick of the second hand dragged like it was wading through tar. Around me, guys traded like nothing had changed, but there was an edge to the room. Everyone knew something was up.

By noon, I was still waiting for any sign of fallout. *Something* had to happen. I could picture those smug bastards sweating it out under questioning, their excuses crumbling as the CME investigators grilled them.

Brad walked up to me between trades, his jaw tight. "They pulled Seth in, huh? You think they're finally gonna hammer him?"

"Maybe," I said, though I didn't sound as confident as I wanted to. "They've got the evidence. It's right there in black and white."

Brad let out a harsh laugh. "Evidence means nothing if they don't want to see it."

I didn't argue, though his words sat like a stone in my gut.

By the end of the day, I still hadn't heard a word. No announcements. No shakeups. Nothing. I watched Will and Lenny stroll back onto the floor like they'd just been out for a long lunch, their grins as smug as ever. Seth slithered in right after them, his demeanor calm. Like nothing had happened. The knot in my stomach twisted tighter and the noise from the CME grew deafening. The tension on the floor simmered, unspoken but ever-present.

Brad was the first to snap. "Screw this." He slammed his trading cards down on the desk beside me, the sound cracked like a gunshot. Papers fluttered, but Brad didn't care. His face was flushed as anger radiated off him. "If the CME won't do a damn thing, I'll take Seth straight to arbitration."

I looked up from my trades, startled but not surprised. "Are you sure about that?"

"Positive," he shot back, his voice as hard as steel. I knew nothing would sway him now. "I'm not gonna sit here and let them skim off me anymore. Arbitration will force him to answer."

I held his gaze for a moment. The resolve in his eyes was unmistakable. "I'm with you, Brad."

"Good." He grabbed his jacket in one quick motion, as if the decision had lit a fire under him. "Let's see how Seth talks his way out of this one."

I watched him storm out, the determination in his steps made it clear that he wasn't bluffing. For the first time in days, it felt like someone was finally taking a swing. The brief momentum quieted as the day dragged on, and the hum of the trading floor turned dull in my ears. During a small break, when the chaos dimmed just enough for me to breathe, Dave appeared at my side.

"Michael," he said quietly. I turned to face him and caught his smirk disappearing under a mask.

"What's up, Dave?"

He forced an apologetic smile, like he was trying too hard to look sincere. "Just wanted to say... about the wedding thing—"

I raised an eyebrow, waiting. "Yeah?"

Dave shifted on his feet, running a hand through his hair. "Look, I shouldn't have acted like that and I'm sorry."

His words sounded right, but the way he delivered them felt wrong. I watched him closely, noticing the flicker of discomfort he couldn't quite hide. He wouldn't meet my eyes and his gaze darted over my shoulder instead.

"It's fine. Forget about it. The wedding was so long ago, anyway."

But I couldn't shake the feeling that his apology wasn't the real reason he'd come over and I had a good guess what it was. By now, word of the complaint must've traveled, Dave knew we'd reported the after-hours trading and dual trades.

"Look, kid," Dave's rich accent cut through my thoughts. He stalked closer to me, trying to close the distance between us, his eyes locked onto mine with an intensity that didn't quite match the words coming out of his mouth. "I don't want things to be different between us. Not on the floor, not off it. I want us to stay cool, you know?" He paused, letting his words hang between us for a second, and I couldn't help but notice the way his fingers twitched, like he was trying to control something.

Was it a nervous tick, or maybe just his mounting discomfort?

"I mean, I taught you the ropes here," he continued. "You wouldn't have made it this far without me. And I want us to keep that kind of relationship, one built on trust. You know, the kind where we've got each other's backs, no matter what."

"Yeah, sure, Dave. We're good," I replied, although I could tell it was with less enthusiaism than he would have liked.

He didn't miss a beat, his smile stretched wide. It was the kind of smile you give someone when you're trying too hard and hiding something you don't want them to see. The kind that never reached your eyes. And right then, I knew he had other intentions.

"So, as your friend and confidant," Dave continued, his voice now lowered to a whisper, "if there's anything you want to tell me, anything you're worried about or thinking about, then please, go ahead and tell me now."

I stood stunned, trying to process what he'd just said. The words hit me like a punch in the gut. My first instinct was to laugh it off, but something about the way Dave was looking at me, and the way he was standing with that insincere grimace, made the whole thing feel wrong. He wasn't here to make peace; he was fishing for information and I wasn't about to spill anything.

I couldn't.

There was too much at stake. We were still waiting to see what the CME would do, and until we had some kind of confirmation, it was too risky to say anything. I wasn't about to give him any insight into what we'd been working on. I didn't trust him, not now, not after everything that had happened. If he really knew what was going on, he'd be more careful, and more guarded.

"Dave..." I started, the words barely leaving my mouth before I took a deep breath and forced a slight smile. "There's nothing to talk about."

The silence stretched between us, and for a moment, it felt like we were playing some kind of mind game, both of us trying to figure out the other. Dave's smile faltered for just a split second before he recovered.

"Yeah, of course," he said, as if he'd expected that answer, like he'd already calculated how I'd respond. "No pressure, Mike. Just thought I'd give you the chance to talk. You know, as a friend."

But there was no warmth in his words, no real sincerity. Just the same practiced indifference. He gave me a tight nod, his eyes lingering on mine just a second too long, before turning on his heel and walking away. I watched him leave, and a cold feeling settled deep in my chest. Something about that conversation, it wasn't just about the wedding, or about us being 'good.' It was about control. He wanted to see what I knew or what I might say.

The bastard knows something. I'm sure of it.

As he disappeared down the hall, I couldn't shake the feeling that the more I saw of Dave, the more I realized he was far from being the 'friend' he claimed to be. And now, I was more certain than ever: If we were going to win this fight, I couldn't afford to trust anyone in the pit.

After a few successful trades, the bell rang to signal the end of the day. Men and women began to file out and I couldn't tell if it was guilt, suspicion, or a little bit of both, but one thing was clear: The floor wasn't just business as usual anymore. Lines were being drawn, sides were being chosen, and I wasn't sure who I could trust. Owen and I walked to the entrance of the building, our yellow jackets standing out like a sore thumb on the grey Chicago streets.

"Still nothing," he muttered. "I don't get it. How can they ignore this? The evidence is right there."

Before I could answer, Brad stormed out of the building, his face a mask of anger and disbelief. He stopped in front of us and let out a bitter laugh.

"Fucking unbelievable!" he spat towards the CME building.

"What happened?" I demanded.

Brad looked at me hard. "I just came from arbitration. You know what I just found out?"

I waited as dread pooled in my mind.

"They're backing him," Brad spat. "The exchange *supports* these practices. Said it's part of how the system 'balances itself.'"

Owen froze. "They're *what*?"

"Yeah," Brad hissed. "They're protecting them. The holding orders, the after-hours trades—it's all just 'part of the process,' according to them."

The floor had always been a ruthless place, but I never thought the exchange would come out and defend this kind of garbage. We had the evidence and it didn't matter because the powerful protected their own.

Owen looked at me for answers. "So what do we do now?"

For the first time, I was lost for words. My eyes wandered around the city of Chicago and I wondered if anyone knew that the trading floor, like the rest of the world, was corrupt.

After all we did, nothing had changed.

Brad shook his head, rage still burning in his eyes. "We'll stop them, Mike. One way or another. This isn't over."

Doubt filled my mind as I watched Will Lawrence laugh with a gaggle of men across the street, untouched and unbothered by the events that had unfolded. I felt the blood rush to my face. The anger simmered over uncontrollably and I had the sudden urge to walk over to them and start throwing punches, but I took a deep breath instead and calmed myself.

"You're right, Brad. This is far from fucking over."

CHAPTER TWELVE

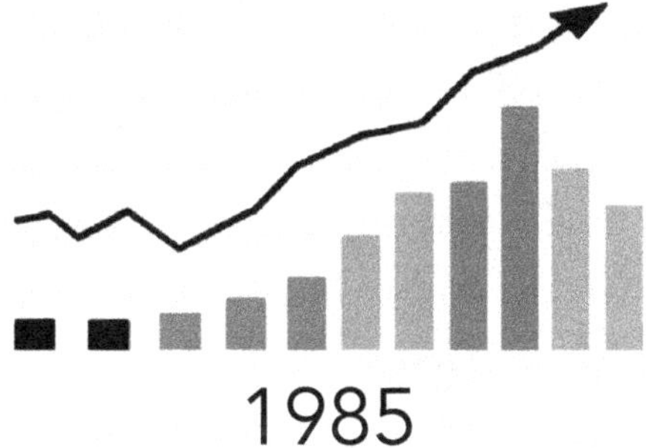

1985

It's a good time to be a trader.

The market had boomed and traders barked out orders as their hands flashed in frantic gestures to get a piece of the cake. The CME was a world unto itself, a melting pot of ambition and aggression where traders of every background fought for their slice of the market. Irish, Italian, Jewish, Polish, the floor was a map of Chicago's immigrant history condensed into a few square feet, each group holding tight to its own.

I leaned against a railing, watching the organized bedlam unfold. A knot of Irish traders crowded one corner, laughing loudly as they ribbed each other between trades. A group of Polish traders stood nearby, their conversation clipped and tense as they strategized. In the middle, an Italian man—like me—was arguing with a Jewish broker. Their roars cut through the rest of the noise like a blade.

"Let me guess." Owen slid up next to me with yellow sleeves rolled up and a bead of sweat on his brow. "They're fighting over who's got the biggest ego this time?"

"Probably," I muttered. "Or maybe just who's got the better lunch spot."

He snorted, but his eyes didn't leave the quarreling men. "I swear, the CME is the only place where you've got to trade futures and abandon your humanity at the same time."

He wasn't wrong. The high-stakes environment of the CME made the Chicago Board of Trade look like a Sunday picnic. There, traders shared similar backgrounds and spoke the same language, figuratively and literally. Here, every difference felt magnified, every stereotype wielded like a weapon. It didn't take much to turn friendly competition into outright hostility.

I noticed one of the younger traders, a wiry Italian guy named Marco, shove past a Polish trader. The older man stumbled slightly but caught himself, glaring after Marco.

"You got a problem, *dupek*?" he growled, his accent thick.

Marco spun around, throwing up his hands. "What the fuck did you just call me?"

"Why you pushing me, huh?"

"You're standing in my damn way!"

"Maybe if you paid attention, you wouldn't need someone to move for you," the Polish trader shot back.

"Hey! Keep it down over there!" one of the brokers barked, but his tone was halfhearted. Everyone knew tensions like these weren't going anywhere.

I sighed and turned back to Owen. "How the hell are we supposed to unite these guys against the brokers when they can't even stand next to each other without throwing insults?"

He rubbed the back of his neck, frowning. "It's like trying to herd cats. Angry, competitive cats with a superiority complex."

"You'd think with how much money's at stake, they'd be willing to set this crap aside," I said, shaking my head.

But deep down, I knew better. On the floor, money was king, but pride came in a close second. Just then, Brad stormed past us, his jaw clenched.

"You see what's going on over there?" he hissed, jerking his thumb toward a huddle of brokers. "They're laughing at us, Mike. Laughing because they know we'll never get it together."

"They won't be laughing for long," I said, though I knew they were probably just laughing at a personal joke and it was just Brad's paranoia.

Uniting these traders against dual trading was starting to feel impossible. It wasn't just about exposing the brokers, it was about convincing everyone here that we had more to gain together than apart.

But how do we bridge a gap when no one's willing to take the first step?

Lately, the energy on the floor had shifted as frustrations hit a breaking point. Traders like Brad, Owen, and a handful of others began to openly question the brokers' practices. The alliance we'd started was gaining ground. Word spread fast about our efforts to overthrow dual trading—and other fraudulent acts of the brokers and their bagmen—and more traders had joined us.

I was settling a trade when suddenly Brad stormed past me, his face a storm cloud of anger.

"Oh, fuck!" I cussed loudly.

He was approaching the two brokers that were chuckling and Seth Kaufman was among them.

"You think we're blind?" Brad shouted, pointing directly at the smirking brokers. "We know exactly what you're doing."

All heads turned. The brokers stopped laughing and looked at Brad, the looks on their faces more amused than threatened.

"You got proof?" he shot back, crossing his arms. "Go ahead, bring it to the CME. See how far that gets you." They burst into laughter again, which made Brad even more furious.

He jabbed a finger into one of the broker's chests. "You hold orders, you trade for your own accounts first, and you think we don't see it? We see everything—and soon the whole world is going to see. If the CME won't do anything about it, then the public will."

The men looked anxiously at each other until Seth chuckled and patted their shoulders.

"Brad, Brad," he said smoothly. "You've got such an imagination. Maybe all that yelling is just messing with your math."

Brad took a step closer and I took that as my cue to stop him. His fists were clenched and ready. "You laugh now, Kaufman, but we're coming for you. For all of you."

I weaved through the crowd as fast as I could to Brad's side.

"Let it go," I said under my breath, grabbing his arm.

He turned to me, his face red with frustration. "Let it go? Are you serious, Michael? These guys are robbing everyone in plain sight, and we're supposed to just take it?"

"No," I said quietly, glancing at the brokers who were still smirking. "But this isn't the place to do it. They want you to lose your cool. Don't give them the satisfaction."

Brad pulled his arm free, muttering under his breath, but he didn't escalate further. He shot one last glare at the brokers before stalking off. I turned back to them, meeting their eyes. My silent glare wasn't submission, it was strategy. They didn't need to know what we were planning or how far we were willing to go. By now, traders around us were whispering furiously, the air thick with tension. Owen caught up to me as I returned to my trades.

"That was risky," he said.

"Brad's always risky, but he's not wrong either," I replied. "Maybe it is time to take it public and see where it goes."

Owen scanned the floor. "You sure about that, Mike?"

I watched Brad pacing near the edge of the pit.

"I'm sure," I said, more to myself than to Owen. "One way or another, we'll get it."

I tried to push the confrontation out of my mind and focus on trading. I dove back in, concentrating on making the right calls and keeping my emotions in check. But even as I scribbled my trades on my card, I noticed that the brokers weren't just laughing anymore, they were moving.

I caught sight of Dave coming my way. His expression seemed calm, but his eyes locked on me like a predator. As he stepped into my space, his voice was low enough that only I could hear.

"You think you're some kind of hero, Russo?" he spat. "This isn't about right or wrong, it's about who wins. And trust me, it's not going to be your little group of vigilantes. If you asked me, Michael, I would've told you to ditch these men and celebrate your own successes. You're winning out here and these bastards, like Brad, are gonna bring you down."

I chuckled in disbelief. "Dave, I'm not you. I grew up learning to have integrity in my personal and work life. I just want to stop the bullshit and you know what's going on here as much as I do."

"You've got no idea how this game works, do you? You're not fighting the system, Russo—you're fighting us. And we play dirty. If you're smart, you'll drop this. Focus on your trades and stay in your lane, kid."

Dave backed off and looked smug. "But hey, you've always been a fast learner. Guess we'll see how far you get with this too."

He walked away and I glared at his back. His usual threats held no power over me. I knew that every move I made was being watched by Dave and the other brokers so I refocused on the numbers in front of me and put the drama on hold. There was not much we could do. After our report to the CME, traders began whispering about how the brokers were flexing their muscles, using their connections within the CME to block any investigation into dual trading.

"They've got the compliance guys in their pockets," Steve muttered to Owen at one of our meetings.

Vince chimed in, "Nothing's going to happen. They'll sweep this under the rug just like they always do."

I clenched my fists at the memory.

We'd worked so hard, gathered so much evidence, and for what?

I snapped out of my thoughts and turned toward the voice. It was Brad, his face flushed from the intensity of the pit. I tucked the card away. The numbers were supposed to bring clarity, but today they only added to the noise.

"In!" I called back, raising my hand to signal. "Five contracts, 252.50!"

Brad nodded, relaying the order instantly to the broker. The pit swallowed me whole again as the roar of voices demanded my attention. But even as I rejoined the chaos, the gap on my card lingered in my mind, like a loose thread waiting to unravel everything.

As the day progressed, the energy in the pit grew more chaotic. The market was fluctuating violently, but for me, the real battle was taking place off the charts. I could feel the tension mounting. Every time I focused on a trade, something went wrong. Orders were delayed, trades were mishandled, and profits slipped through my fingers. It was no coincidence.

I glanced over at Seth. I knew that he and some brokers were making moves to take me down. Every misstep I made felt like it was their doing. I'd never been a quitter, though, and I wasn't about to start now. The more they tried to not trade with me, the harder I pushed back.

I stood by the post when Brad came up to me, glancing over his shoulder to make sure no one was listening. "They're gunning for you, Mikey. It's them. They're trying to sabotage you."

I kept my eyes fixed ahead. "I know. It's happening more every day."

Brad's jaw tightened, his frustration obvious. "You think they're gonna let this go on much longer? You think they're gonna just back off because we're keeping records and pointing out what they're doing? They'll bury you if they have to."

I met his eyes, my resolve hardening. "If we back down, they win. Nothing changes, Brad. And I won't let them win."

"Just be careful. These guys aren't playing fair. They've got the CME wrapped around their dirty fingers."

Before I could respond, Owen appeared with a grim expression. "Mike, I get it. I do. But we need to think this through. These brokers, they're not gonna let up. And they've got the CME on their side."

I ran a hand through my hair. "What do you want me to do, Owen? Let them walk all over us?"

Owen looked around, ensuring no one else was close enough to hear. "I'm saying, maybe it's time to lay low for a bit. Keep our heads down until we have something concrete, something they can't ignore."

"I can't do that."

Owen's eyes darkened, and so did his voice. "Mike, you have a wife to take care of, and who knows? Maybe even a baby soon. They'll destroy you and your family if they can. You're walking a fine line here. These guys play dirty, and they don't care who gets caught in the crossfire."

His words stung, but I knew he was right. The brokers had more power than we could ever have imagined, and the CME wasn't exactly rushing to intervene. I would rather lose trades than lose Shannon. But if I didn't stand my ground then everything we'd worked for would mean nothing. My mind was a mess with these contradictory thoughts.

Nevertheless, the day was coming to an end and I couldn't wait to get home to my wife and leave the pit behind for the night. Just as the bell rang, a broker stopped us from leaving our places.

"Hold up," he called, glancing around as if to make sure no one else was in earshot. "Got an announcement for all you successful independents and brokers," he said.

"We're planning something special." He grinned slyly. "Call it a vacation. You know, to get away from all this noise." He motioned vaguely around the pit. "Only the ones who show up will know when and where *The Filth Open* will be held."

A hush fell over the group of traders standing nearby, their interest piqued, but this invitation didn't sit right with me.

"A vacation with these dickheads? I'll be there!" Brad yelled from somewhere in the crowd.

He responded with chuckles but I was too lost in the weight of the announcement. "The Filth Open?" I muttered under my breath. "What kind of name is that?" It felt like a veiled threat, a power move designed to separate the real players from the ones who might be standing in their way.

The broker's grin widened as if he could read our skepticism. "You'll know when the time comes," he said, and with that, he turned and disappeared into the crowd, leaving behind an uneasy tension.

This wasn't just some casual get-together. The brokers weren't known for doing anything without a purpose. And the timing? It couldn't have been more suspect.

"They're up to something," Owen said as if he read my thoughts.

I couldn't agree more.

CHAPTER THIRTEEN

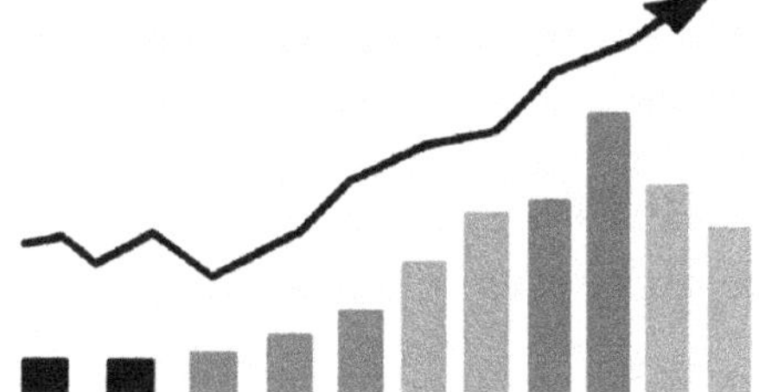

The gravel crunched under the tires as the car came to a stop in front of the sprawling estate of the White Oak Farms. The place looked like something straight out of a movie—a pristine golf course stretched into the distance, bordered by perfectly manicured hedges. The main building stood proudly in the center, a towering castle-like building with enormous glass windows. It was the kind of place where you'd expect to sit back and not argue about trades.

"Holy hell, look at this place," Brad muttered, leaning out of the car window as he whistled. "Think they've got room service? Maybe a private jet tucked out back?"

"Yeah, Brad," I said, grabbing my bag from the trunk. "I'm sure they'll have the concierge drive you to the tee in a Rolls."

Steve stumbled out of the back seat, already holding a flask. He tilted it toward me with a grin. "Rolls or not, I'm getting trashed before dinner. Cheers to living like kings!"

"Steve," Vince sighed, shaking his head as he slung his golf bag over one shoulder. "You're already drunk, you idiot. Try to keep it together until after we unpack."

Steve took a swig, swaying a little on his feet. "Who says I'm drunk? I'm just... warming up. This is prep work. You wouldn't show up to the floor unprepared, would you?"

"Yeah, well, you keep 'prepping,' and you're going to end up face-down on the green before we even start," Vince shot back.

As the banter carried on, Owen spoke over them. "Relax, Mike. It's a vacation weekend. You could use a break."

I grunted as I adjusted my bag. "A weekend with these guys? After that road trip? Relaxing is the last thing I'll be doing."

"Hey!" Brad spun around. "That was a bonding experience! Nothing brings guys together like being crammed into a car for hours with Steve's farts.'"

"Bonding experience?" I laughed. "Brad, we almost left you at the gas station when you wouldn't stop talking about your trades from '82. And Steve's playlist was just three hours of Van Halen on repeat!"

Steve pointed his flask at me. "Don't you dare insult Van Halen, young man. That's sacrilegious. I oughta make you walk to the lodge for that."

Owen chuckled as he walked ahead, waving his hand at the grandeur surrounding us. "You guys can argue about music later. Look at this place! Fresh air, open skies... doesn't get better than this, and we need this break."

I looked around, taking it in. There was something unsettling about how perfect everything looked. A group of traders and brokers mingled near the lodge, laughing and gesturing animatedly, but the undertone felt off, like the forced camaraderie you see before a fight.

"Yeah," I said under my breath, hoisting my bag higher on my shoulder. "Doesn't get better than this."

Steve staggered forward, flask still in hand. "Mark my words, boys. By the end of this weekend, I'll be the king of this damn farm. Now, who's carrying my bag?"

"Carry it yourself, you drunk bastard," Vince muttered, giving him a light shove as we headed toward the lodge.

The weekend had barely started, and already, I could feel the chaos brewing.

The dining hall at the Club was nothing short of opulent. Crystal chandeliers hung above the expansive room, soft light reflecting off pristine white tablecloths and polished silverware. Waitstaff in crisp uniforms weaved through the crowd, serving dishes that looked more like art than food. The brokers, loud and boisterous as always, were already three drinks in by the time we sat down. Dave, positioned at the head of the table like a king, raised his glass.

"To a weekend of success, gentlemen! And to knowing the right people." He shot a pointed look at me before downing his scotch.

Owen leaned over and whispered. "What does that even mean? 'The right people?' The guy probably bribed his way into his first job."

I smirked. "Careful, Owen. Or you might end up disappearing at this resort.'"

"Not a chance. I'll fuck each of them up and leave them for death."

The courses began rolling out, lobster bisque, filet mignon, and some dessert so fancy I didn't even know how to pronounce it. Meanwhile, the drinks kept flowing. Vince was halfway into a bottle of wine. Steve, who was already drunk before we arrived, started shouting random things about how he could beat anyone at golf, and Brad was quietly dissecting his steak like it owed him money.

Halfway through the meal, Dave stood up with a glass in hand. "You know what I love about this business?" He paused dramatically, waiting for someone to take the bait.

"Exploiting people?" Brad said loudly, earning a round of laughter from our end of the table. Dave's grin tightened, but he ignored the jest.

"It's the camaraderie. Nights like this, where we can forget about the floor and just enjoy the fruits of our labor."

"Fruits of *your* labor," I muttered under my breath. Owen snorted, nearly choking on his drink.

As the night wore on, the mood grew rowdier. Dave made sure no one's glass was empty, and by dessert, most of the table was either drunk, belligerent, or both. When the waiter discreetly handed Owen a small leather folder, he frowned and opened it. His face paled.

"What the hell is this?"

Dave walked over, all charm and smarm.

"Oh, that? Just the bill for tonight's festivities."

Owen's eyes widened in disbelief. "This says $8,500! What the actual hell, Dave? You said this was your treat! I thought the brokers had it covered."

"Yeah with *our* money," Brad said sarcastically.

Dave leered at them. "Consider it an investment in our friendship, Owen."

"An investment? You're out of your damn mind!" Owen looked around the table as his voice rose. "Who orders *five* bottles of Dom Pérignon? I didn't even drink any of it!"

Steve swayed slightly in his chair and raised his hand. "That was me. Thought it'd pair well with the caviar."

"It's *steak*, not caviar, you idiot!" Owen snapped, throwing his napkin on the table.

Brad butted in. "Hey, at least now you've got a great story, Owen. 'The Night Dave Screwed Me Over in Style... again.'"

"Real funny, Brad," Owen muttered as he glared at Dave, who looked like he couldn't care less. "I'm not paying this."

"Relax," Dave said smoothly. "Expense it. It's not like you're hurting for cash."

Owen looked ready to throttle him, and this was my cue to butt in.

"Owen, he's not worth it."

He groaned and sank back into his chair. "This weekend's already a damn disaster."

On the other side of the room, the brokers roared with laughter as the waiter whisked the bill away and Dave toasted yet again, his glass raised high. I just shook my head and took in the scene. The weekend had barely begun, and already, the knives were out, just hidden behind faux smiles and expensive scotch.

The evening descended into madness faster than I thought possible. After the $8,500 dinner debacle, most of the attendees had loosened up, or, more accurately, lost all sense of decorum. The brokers were in rare form, and just when I thought the night couldn't get any more absurd, the same slimy broker from the pit's announcement stood on a makeshift stage near the bar and tapped his glass for attention.

"Gentlemen," he began, with a smirk like he'd just pulled off the scam of the century. "The time has come. The *Filth Open* starts tonight. If you're here, you're part of the family now."

The crowd erupted into cheers, whistles, and applause. I exchanged a look with Owen, who looked like he wasn't sure whether to laugh or vomit.

"What the hell does that even mean?" I asked Brad.

"You'll see."

And that was all he said before the doors on the far end of the room swung open and in sauntered a parade of naked women. The room exploded in a racket of howls, whistles, and laughter as the women strutted through the crowd like it was the most normal thing in the world.

"Mike, this is insane," Owen said, but his eyes wandered helplessly over the exposed tits and asses.

"Insane?" I replied, shaking my head in disbelief. "This is disgusting."

Owen's attention, however, was quickly diverted by a brunette with legs that seemed to stretch for miles. She winked at him, and that was all it took. He stood, straightened his tie, and followed her like a moth to a flame.

"Owen," I called after him, "she's not going to help you pay off that dinner bill!"

He waved me off without looking back. "Priorities, Mike!"

Meanwhile, I stayed rooted to my spot, trying to make sense of the insanity around me. Seth sidled up to me, drink in hand and a smug expression plastered across his face.

"Hell of a show, isn't it?" he said, gesturing to the chaos around us. "This is what success looks like, Russo. You've got potential. Don't waste it by staying on the outside."

I gave him a tight smile. "Thanks for the pep talk, but I'm fine where I am."

Seth's expression hardened. "Suit yourself. But don't say we didn't offer."

He sauntered off, leaving me to stew in the mess around me. The brokers weren't just here for the debauchery, they were playing a longer game.

Were they trying to pull me into their web?

As the party spiraled further into madness—with drugs, alcohol, and slurred shouts echoing through the halls—I couldn't shake the feeling that I was being watched. Brad disappeared, Steve was passed out on the carpeted floor, and Vince made his way to the bar. Owen, meanwhile, was fully enthralled by his new "friend." I spotted him in the corner, gesturing wildly as the brunette whispered something in his ear and kissed his neck. I decided to head back to my hotel room and was just passing by when Steve jolted awake, drunk out of his mind.

"Mike," he slurred, "this place... this place is heaven, isn't it? Look, naked angels."

"If heaven involves STDs and bankruptcy, then sure," I replied dryly.

He cackled and quickly passed out again. I shook my head and made my way back to my room but the sounds of moans in the hallway were loud enough to keep a neighborhood awake.

I wouldn't be able to sleep in this raucous.

I walked past my door and headed to the bar instead, hoping to clear my mind. The dim lighting and quiet hum of conversation were a welcome reprieve from the madness I'd left behind. At the far end of the bar, I spotted Ronnie locked in an intense make-out session with some brunette. He was completely oblivious to my presence, but that changed when he finally came up for air. He was glassy-eyed from the amount of cocaine he snorted.

"What do you think of the chick I'm with, Mikey?" he yelled.

I took a closer look, and my jaw dropped.

"Ronnie," I said slowly, "that's not a chick. That's a guy."

Ronnie blinked at me, then turned back to his "date," his face a mixture of confusion and horror as realization dawned on him. I bit back a laugh.

"What the fuck! Get out of my face you bastard!" Ronnie waved his hands around haphazardly as if chasing a fly, the man got up and left, swinging his hair dramatically. I couldn't hold back my laughter, it rolled out of me until tears pricked at the corner of my eyes.

"Well, shit!" Ronnie shouted. "I was about to fuck him!"

"Don't worry," I said through my laughter. "Your secret's safe with me, Ronnie. For now." It was the first moment of levity I'd had all night, and as I sat at the bar, I couldn't help but laugh to myself.

After a glass of whiskey I debated heading back to my room and calling it a night. But I figured I should at least check on the guys in case they weren't passed out somewhere—or worse.

The private hall pulsed with music behind the closed double doors, and muffled laughter and shouts spilled out into the corridor. Bracing myself, I pushed one of the doors open and stepped inside. The sight that greeted me was straight out of hell.

Men and women were entangled across plush sofas, their clothes completely discarded. The air was thick with smoke, sex, alcohol, and something far stronger. Trays of cocaine were scattered across tables, and a few guys were slumped over, noses still pressed against the remnants. In one corner, a broker I vaguely recognized was snorting a line off a prostitute's ass. In another, a group of men had circled around a loveseat where two women were putting on a performance I definitely hadn't signed up for.

"What the fuck..." I muttered under my breath.

As I scanned the room, I finally spotted Brad, Vince, and Steve at a round table in the center. Owen was nowhere to be found.

"Brad!" I called.

He turned to me drunkenly with a grin, "Mike! You made it! Thought you bailed on the fun."

"This is fun?" I gestured to the madness around us. "I think we have very different definitions of the word."

"Don't be such a goddamn buzzkill," Brad said, chuckling. "It's not every day you get invited to the Filth Open. Live a little."

"Yeah, Mike." Steve barely managed to keep himself upright. "You need to get laid or something. Relax! We're all gonna die someday!"

"I'm married, and so are you," I shot back. "Seriously, this is insane. You don't see a problem with any of this?"

Brad shrugged, but his grin faded slightly. "Look, it's not exactly my scene either, but you gotta play the game, man. You don't want these guys thinking you're better than them."

"I *am* better than this," I said firmly.

Vince finally spoke up, his voice low. "I think Mike's right. This is a whole new level of messed up."

"Thank you," I said, pointing at Vince. "At least someone still has their brain intact."

Before Brad could respond, a loud cheer erupted from across the room. One of the prostitutes had climbed onto the table, holding a champagne bottle aloft like a trophy, while the men around her chanted and egged her on.

"Unbelievable," I muttered, shaking my head.

"Don't worry, Mike," Steve said, leaning back in his chair. "You don't have to join in. Just enjoy the view!"

"That's it," I said, throwing up my hands. "I'm out. Good luck surviving this shit show."

I made my way back to the hotel as fast as I could. The quiet was a relief, but my mind was still reeling from everything I'd seen.

If this is what it takes to succeed, then I want no part of it.

I sat on the edge of the bed and then reached for the phone. Shannon's voice was the only thing that could ground me right now.

She picked up on the second ring. "Hey, baby. Everything okay?"

"Yeah," I said, though my voice sounded tired. "I just... miss you. A lot."

She paused for a moment. "I miss you too. What's going on?"

"It's nothing. I just wanted to hear your voice."

"Well, I'm here," she said, "You'll be home soon, right?"

"Yeah... soon."

CHAPTER FOURTEEN

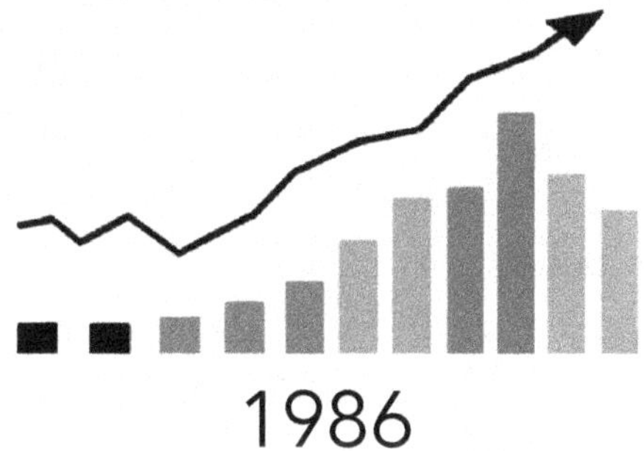

1986

The night air chilled the streets as we pulled up to Chicago Stadium, our usual haunt for escaping the madness of the CME. The buzz around Michael Jordan was addictive. It was only his third season, but the way he moved on the court, you knew the guy was destined for the Bulls. We got in just as the first quarter ended. Owen always joked about how getting there late saved us from overpriced beers during warmups. Vince smirked as he handed over his ticket.

"Yeah, because scalping for a seat is *so* economical," he muttered.

Inside, the energy was palpable. Jordan had the ball, weaving past defenders like they were planted in cement. The crowd roared as he leapt for an impossible dunk.

"Jesus, look at him," Vince said, nudging me. "Kid's got more moves than Dave Patterson during a CFTC audit."

I chuckled. "Difference is Jordan's playing fair."

Steve was already a few beers deep by the time we found our seats. "You know," he slurred, leaning slightly on Owen, "if I was six inches taller, I'd be the guy down there dunking. Hell, give me another beer, and I'll show you how it's done."

"Yeah, Steve," Owen quipped, "maybe after halftime, when you've got *Jordan-level* coordination from all that Budweiser." The second quarter passed in a blur of no-look passes, three-pointers, and Jordan stealing the show.

By halftime, the ritual kicked in. We filed out and headed to our regular spot for drinks, leaving the diehard fans behind. At the bar, the conversation turned, as it always did, back to the trading floor.

Vince tipped his beer toward me. "You know, Mike, we oughta bring some of that Jordan magic into the pit. Dunk over the brokers for once."

"Yeah," I replied. "But the floor's no game. There's no ref blowing the whistle on their bullshit."

We could talk about trading until the morning, and that's exactly what we did. By the time we called it a night, it was past two in the morning. Steve stumbled into a cab, muttering something about strategy for his trades tomorrow. When we saw him the next day, the real entertainment began. Cynthia had apparently been waiting for him when he got home. She cornered him in the kitchen, arms crossed and unloaded.

"Where the hell have you been, Steve?"

Steve, quick on his feet despite the hangover, fired back, "Relax, honey. The game went into overtime."

Owen doubled over laughing when he heard that story but even as we laughed, my mind wandered back to Jordan. The guy was out there making history, turning chaos into beauty. Meanwhile, we were just trying to survive in the murky waters of the CME, where the rules were as clear as mud and fairness was as rare as an empty bar on Rush Street.

The morning after the Bulls game, I walked into the CME building to an atmosphere crackling with tension. The usual chaos of the trading floor; calls to buy or sell, the clattering of tickets, and the sharp voices of runners, was overshadowed by a palpable unease. Traders clustered in tight knots, their conversations hushed but intense.

What is going on now?

As I settled into my booth, Vince hurried over, his face uncharacteristically pale. He stooped toward me, glanced around like he was afraid someone might overhear, and then asked, "Mike, have you seen it?"

"Seen what?" I already dreaded the answer.

Vince shoved a folded photograph into my hands. My stomach turned as I took in the image: a group of familiar faces from "The Filth Open," drinks in hand, surrounded by naked women.

"There's more," Vince said and handed me more photos.

The shots showed a table piled with cocaine. In the corner, Owen stood with a dazed expression and a prostitute draped over his lap. In another, Steve was laughing uproariously while holding a bottle of Dom Pérignon. A scantily clad woman stood next to him and his free hand was clasped around her tit.

"Holy shit!" I hissed.

Owen appeared next, red-faced from embarrassment. I assumed he saw the pictures too. When he reached me he gripped my arm like a drowning man clinging to a life raft. His eyes were wild.

"Jesus, Mike. This could ruin me! Do you know what this looks like? I've got a family, a reputation—"

Steve wasn't far behind, his usually cheerful demeanor replaced with a sweaty, panicked look. "If Cynthia sees this, I'm a dead man. Forget trading—I'll be divorced before lunch. Shit, what the hell was I thinking?" He buried his face in his hands before shooting upright, his voice rising. "Wait. This has to be illegal, right? Who took these photos? Someone's gotta pay for this!"

I kept my voice low, trying to calm them. "I told you something about that night didn't sit right with me. Now you know why. This wasn't just a party—it was a goddamn trap."

Owen paced the floor, stress lines began to form on his forehead. "Fuck, this is how they're attacking us?"

I glanced toward the brokers' section. Lenny was smirking, watching the chaos slowly unfold before him. Dave stood nearby, exchanging a few quiet words with Will.

They didn't have a care in the world.

"They're playing us," I said grimly. "It's about control with them. They want to discredit us, the independent traders, and keep us in line. If we look bad enough, no one will take us seriously when we fight back against their schemes."

Owen stopped pacing. "So, what do we do? How do we stop this?"

"For now? Keep your head down and don't react," I said. "If they see you panicking, it'll only get worse."

Steve groaned, dropping into a chair. "Great advice, Mike. Just ignore the fact that my wife's gonna get a copy of this and murder me in my sleep."

Despite the tension, I couldn't help but smirk. "Well, Steve, maybe next time you'll think twice about partying like it's your last night on Earth."

"Ha ha, real fuckin' funny," he snapped, throwing a pen at me.

Owen rubbed his face aggressively as if trying to wake up from a bad dream. "This is bad, Mike. Really bad."

"I know. But panicking won't help. If we give up now, they win."

I glanced back at the brokers' section, where their smug looks hadn't faded and my resolve hardened.

This is blackmail.

Suddenly Brad came striding onto the floor, grinning from ear to ear like he'd just hit the jackpot.

"Gentlemen!" he announced loudly, clapping his hands together. His booming voice caught the attention of several men around them. "Big news. I just locked down five more guys for the alliance. That makes twenty-five of us. We've got numbers now. We're unstoppable!"

No one reacted. Not a single word. Owen stared at the floor like it might swallow him whole, and Steve just kept muttering under his breath about his impending divorce. Vince sat at a desk, shoulders slumped like he'd aged ten years in ten minutes.

Brad stopped in his tracks and his smile faltered. "What the hell is wrong with you guys? This is good news! We're finally getting somewhere."

I sighed and handed him the photos. "Take a look for yourself."

Brad frowned as he looked at the photos, his brow furrowed deeper while he scanned the image as if studying every detail of it. Silence hung heavily in the air while we watched him taking it all in—Owen looking like a deer caught in headlights, Steve in his champagne-fueled glory, and the unmistakable debauchery of *The Filth Open*. For a moment, Brad just stared at it with an unreadable expression.

Then he laughed. And not just a chuckle.

No.

Brad threw his head back and *howled* with laughter.

"You've got to be kidding me!" he managed to gasp between laughs. "This is what's got you all acting like someone died?"

Steve shot him a murderous look. "Oh, I'm sorry, Brad. Did your wife end up in one of these photos? Oh, wait, you're single, so you wouldn't understand."

Brad waved him off, still grinning. "C'mon, Steve, lighten up. This is priceless. I mean, look at Owen's face! It's like he just saw a ghost. And you? Popping bottles like you're in a MTV music video." He turned the paper toward me. "Mike, seriously, tell me this isn't funny."

I crossed my arms. "It's not funny when they're using this to destroy us."

Brad sobered slightly, but the glint in his eye didn't fade. "Alright, fair point. But you've got to admit, these photos are fucking good. Can I keep these? I'll frame it and hang it for motivation."

Owen finally snapped. "This could ruin us, Brad! It's not a joke!"

Brad held up his hands, still holding the photos. "Alright, alright, relax. I get that it's serious stuff. But look, we can't let them see us falling apart over this. That's exactly what they want." He looked at me. "Mike, back me up here."

I responded reluctantly. "He's right. As bad as this looks, panicking isn't going to help. We stick together and stay focused. This is just another move in their game."

Brad smirked. "Exactly. And in the meantime, I'll keep this for safekeeping. You know, in case we need a reminder of why we're doing this."

"Don't you dare," Owen growled.

Brad grinned wider, tucking the photo into his jacket pocket. "Too late."

Despite the tension, I couldn't help the corner of my mouth from twitching upward. Brad had a way of defusing even the worst situations. But that didn't last long. As the morning wore on, a new wave of whispers rippled through the floor, pulling everyone's focus from the photo scandal.

"You hear about the guys in the aqua jackets? They're calling themselves Dolphin Trading. Word is, they're FBI." Vince hovered near us as we all stared at the photographs trying to guess who was who in all of them.

Brad snorted. "FBI? On the floor? Give me a break."

"No, seriously," Vince insisted. "They've been around for a couple of weeks, laying low, but they're asking questions—too many questions. You think they're legit? FBI, here to clean this mess up?"

I considered it for a moment and scanned the floor. It wasn't hard to spot the new guys. Their aqua jackets stood out like a beacon in a sea of bold reds, greens, and yellows. They moved in pairs, always watching, always listening.

"If they are," I said, "they're not here for us. They're here for whoever's at the top. And if that's the case, we might be collateral damage."

Owen looked increasingly pale as he stared at the floor. "Or maybe they're here to set us all up. What if this is some sting operation? What if they're building a case, and we're just pieces on the board?"

Brad rolled his eyes. "You've been watching too many crime dramas, Owen. Look, even if they are FBI, it's not like they're here to drag us out in cuffs. They're after bigger fish, right, Mike?"

I wasn't so sure.

"Depends on how big they think we are."

The conversation left a shadow over the group. The trading pit was a place of constant motion and noise, but today the usual chaos felt heavier with each piece of news we received. It was like everyone was walking on a tightrope and the slightest nudge could send us all plunging.

Steve spoke up and broke the silence. "If this photo thing wasn't bad enough, now we've got the Feds sniffing around? This is a nightmare."

"Keep it together," I said firmly. "If we fall apart now, we're done."

Brad snapped his fingers, the sound sharp enough to jolt us. "Mike's right. Forget about the Dolphins or whatever they call themselves. Let's focus on the plan. Twenty-five strong, remember? That's what matters. We're not going down without a fight."

His optimism was infectious, but we knew we were being watched. Whether it was by the brokers, the so-called Dolphin Trading group, or the CME itself.

What if Owen was right about the FBI?

That question stuck with me as I returned to the pit and watched the screens and tried to end the day on a positive note.

It wasn't just me. Other independents in our group were dealing with the same nonsense every day. It was death by a thousand cuts, and the brokers knew exactly what they were doing. During the storm of the pit, Dave strolled over with his usual polished grin plastered on his face. Behind him, Will followed closely.

Dave stood close to me and said pointedly, "You keep pushing against us, Russo, and you'll break. You join us, and you'll thrive. It's simple math."

"I'd rather break than sell out."

Will's laugh was short and cold. "You might not have a choice. Everyone's got a price, Russo. Or a weakness. Since drugs and booze aren't your weakness, maybe it's that pretty red-haired wife of yours?"

Before I could think about it my arm recoiled. My fist contacted with Will's smug face and sent him spiraling on top of a group of traders. Dave rushed to his aid.

"Woah, woah, woah!" Owen yelled and ran toward us. "What the fuck is going on, Mike?"

I stalked to where Will laid on the ground and squealed like a pig.

Blood pooled in his mouth as I pointed a finger at him and spat, "You ever mention my wife again and I'll fucking kill you. You heard me?"

Dave quickly stepped in between us and placed a hand on my chest. "Easy, Russo," he growled.

I glared at Will, who was still trying to wipe the blood from his mouth, his face contorted in pain and anger. He couldn't seem to decide whether to retaliate or slink away.

I didn't care.

I wasn't about to let anyone threaten my family.

"Don't think you can intimidate me with your cheap shots," I muttered, my fists still clenched at my sides. "You don't know a damn thing about me or what I'm capable of."

Will finally pushed himself up and wiped the blood off his lips with the back of his hand. He glared at me but stayed silent.

"You better keep that temper in check, Russo," Dave warned as they walked back to their post. "You won't get any sympathy from us next time."

My chest heaved with adrenaline as I watched them disappear into the crowd. Owen pulled on my shoulder and guided me back to our spot. As we walked, the men in the blue jackets watched us.

CHAPTER FIFTEEN

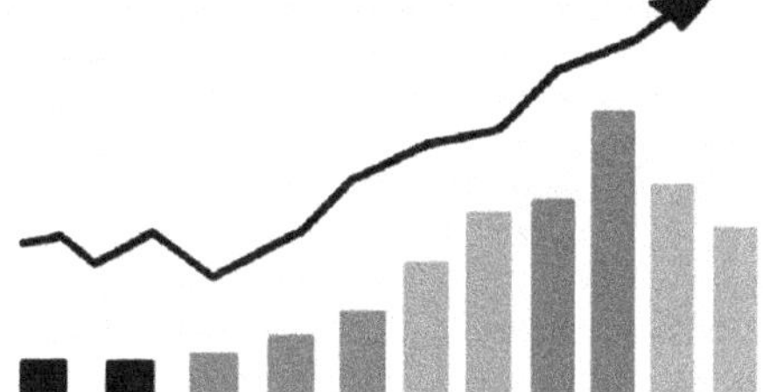

The bar was dimly lit, the kind of place where the jukebox was older than most of the traders crammed around the tables. Owen, Vince, Steve, Brad, and I pushed through the crowd to the back room, where twenty-five independent traders—our growing coalition—were already gathered. The air smelled like stale beer and tension, the kind of atmosphere that could boil over at any moment. Conversations buzzed low until Stan Weinberg, standing at the head of the table, held up a folder and rapped it against his palm.

"Alright, listen up," Stan said, cutting through the noise like a bell. "I've been digging through the CME's bylaws, and I think I've found something we can use."

The room quieted, every face turning toward him. Stan opened the folder and held up a photocopy of a clause in the CME rulebook.

"If we're going to take on dual trading, we need to understand how the CME works. Any major change, like reforming or banning dual trading, has to go through a vote. Every seat-holder gets a say, and believe me, the brokers will be working overtime to protect their interests."

Owen leaned back in his chair, arms crossed. "So, what? We just walk into a meeting and expect them to vote against their own paychecks? That's a long shot."

"Not just a meeting, Owen. A special meeting," Stan clarified. "According to CME bylaws, members can petition for a vote if we gather enough signatures to call one. But here's the kicker: even if we get it on the ballot, we'll need more than just our coalition to win."

"What's stopping them from brushing this off like they always do?" I asked.

Stan smirked and held up a page of the bylaws. "This. Clause 3.7. If we present concrete evidence of manipulation, like the kind we discussed earlier, it'll force the Board to take it seriously. They can't ignore a formal petition backed by evidence."

"Even if they take it seriously," Brad chimed in, "what's stopping the brokers from turning the whole floor against us?"

"Public pressure," Stan replied swiftly. "The CME doesn't exist in a vacuum. If the FBI gets involved or if word leaks to the press, seat-holders might think twice before siding with the brokers. Nobody wants their name tied to a scandal."

Owen whistled low. "So, we're talking evidence, votes, and maybe some public shaming. Got it."

Stan nodded. "Exactly. But we need to play this smart. First, we rally enough members who stand to gain from reforms—other independents, arbitrageurs, even some disillusioned brokers. Then, we hit them with the evidence and make it impossible to say no."

Vince, always a realist, chimed in with a grim tone. "We've tried bringing evidence to the CME before. They brushed it off, said it wasn't substantial enough. What's different this time?"

Stan tapped the folder. "This time, we're not just filing a complaint and hoping for the best. We're building a legal case and playing by the

CME's rules. If they ignore this and the FBI gets wind of it, which I'm assuming they already did, they'll have no choice but to act."

Owen shot a look at me. "And speaking of the Feds, who the hell brought them in? They don't just show up for fun."

"Could've been a client," Kevin, a quieter trader, said. "Maybe someone got burned bad enough they wanted revenge."

"Or a broker tried to cover his ass," Stan added with a shrug. "Hell, it could've been anyone. But what matters is they're here, and that's leverage we didn't have before."

I glanced at the group. Tensions were high, but there was a new kind of energy in the room. Everyone knew this time there was a lot more at stake.

"The plan is simple," I said, standing to command the room's attention. "We continue to gather every piece of evidence we can, delayed trades, misfiled orders, anything that shows manipulation. Stan will work on building our case. The rest of you, keep your heads down and stay united. They can't fight all of us at once."

Brad gave a mock salute. "You know, I was planning on staying low, but now that you've told me to, I'm definitely gonna make a scene."

"Of course you are," Owen muttered. "We're counting on you, Brad, to keep the bar entertained."

"Hey, someone has to do it," Brad grinned. "I mean, I'm already a walking distraction."

Everyone laughed and the mood immediately felt lighter. After an hour of drinking and camaraderie, the traders began to filter out into the Chicago night, some looking determined, and others visibly nervous.

As Owen and I walked to the door, he muttered under his breath, "You think it will work this time, Mike?"

"It has to. We don't have another plan."

Vince caught up to us as we stepped out into the chilly evening. "But seriously, Mike, what if it all falls apart? I mean, we've got Stan on our side, but these brokers are ruthless. What then?"

I rubbed my chin. "Then we fight harder. If they think we're scared, they'll eat us alive."

Brad threw an arm around Vince's shoulder, grinning. "Come on, Vince. You can't be scared. I've got an entire bar of traders ready to riot. What's the worst that could happen?"

Owen raised an eyebrow at Brad. "I'll tell you what's gonna happen. You're gonna get us thrown out of this bar too and we're all gonna have to find a new meeting spot, again."

Brad winked. "It's not a problem if it's not my fault. Just remember that."

"I kinda miss Steve," Vince said so quietly we almost missed it. We murmured in agreement.

"Yeah, that alcoholic fucker. Where is he anyway?" Owen replied.

"Cynthia got him by the balls after those pictures were released," Vince replied.

"Oh, shit! I keep forgetting about those damn pictures." Owen laughed tensely as he remembered their captured debauchery.

"Poor Steve." I truly did sympathize for the old man.

"Jesus fucking Christ, the man's not dead... yet." Brad's witty comment cut through our reveries of Steve and the group burst into laughter.

Our mingled voices echoed through the air, a small but necessary reminder that we were still in this fight together. We walked into the cold as our breath hung in the winter air like smoke. The group began to break off, exchanging hurried goodbyes until, finally, it was just me and Brad left standing on the street corner.

We stood on the street corner, the cold biting at our faces, when Brad turned to me, his hands stuffed in his coat pockets. "So, how you getting home, Mike? Your car still in the shop?"

"Yeah, I'll catch a train."

Brad chuckled. "Always the stubborn one. Owen would've gladly taken you home. But alright, man, you take care. See you tomorrow."

"See you, Brad."

He gave me a quick wave before he walked off into the night. I was left standing alone and staring at the dimly lit street, the harsh winter wind slicing through my jacket. The train station was just a few blocks away, so I walked. The rhythmic sound of my boots on the icy pavement mingled with the distant hum of the city.

It was late and the streets were quieter than usual for a city like Chicago, but I wasn't in the mood to appreciate the stillness. My mind was racing, and I needed some time to think. When I boarded the near-empty train, the smell of stale metal and old upholstery hit me. The fluorescent lights flickered overhead, casting an almost eerie glow over the rows of vacant seats. I sank into one near the door, staring out the window as the train jerked into motion. The city slid past me, its skyline dotted with darkened windows and distant lights that seemed too far away.

As I tried to unwind, I noticed a man standing a few seats away. He wore a fedora and a long, dark trench coat, his figure shadowed by the dim lighting. I could've sworn I saw him earlier, back at the bar during the meeting. Maybe I was imagining things, but the man's presence felt familiar.

I glanced at him again. He wasn't looking directly at me, but the way he was standing too still for too long made my skin crawl. The train rumbled on, the sound of the wheels clattering on the tracks the only noise that filled the otherwise quiet carriage. I shifted uncomfortably in my seat, not sure if the stranger was looking at me or not. I tried not to make eye contact while my instincts screamed at me that this man was dangerous.

Suddenly he stood up and began moving toward the door. I swallowed audibly as he took a few steps down the aisle, his footsteps seemed too deliberate. I tried to ignore it, but I couldn't shake the feeling that he was continuously watching me. The sharp whistle of the departing train distracted me for a second, signaling our approach to the next stop.

I stood quickly as my heart pounded and my eyes scanned the exit. The man was right behind me now, his steps in perfect sync with mine. I could feel his threatening presence approaching my back.

Without thinking, I picked up my pace and tried to get to the door faster. But before I could make it, the man grabbed my arm tightly. I whirled around as adrenaline flooded my veins. He put his hand inside his coat, and my instincts kicked in.

He has a gun.

I ducked just as a gunshot rang out, the loud bang echoed in the confined space. The shot missed me by inches and the force of the bullet grazed the edge of my coat. I sprang into action and dodged another bullet as the man fired again. My heart was pounding painfully in my chest as I ran toward the exit. The sound of my own breath was loud in my ears.

I need to get out of here.

I bolted toward the door, yanking it open and jumping off the train just before it hit the platform. I sprinted through the dark alleyways, the sound of my hurried footsteps mixed with the distant wail of the train's whistle. I took a shortcut through the side streets, adrenaline pushing me faster than I should've been going, until I found myself at the back of my house. I shoved the door open and slid through the backyard and into the kitchen.

Shannon was there, looking up from the stove, her face lit up when she saw me. "Mike, what happened? Why are you—"

Before she could finish, I ran to our bookshelf and pulled out the gun I kept there for our safety.

"Someone tried to kill me." I cocked the gun and checked outside every window but found no one.

Shannon's expression was cold. "What? Who?"

"I don't know." My mind raced. "I think it was a hit, but I don't know why. Could've been the brokers, could've been someone else."

Shannon came over and grabbed my free hand, which was shaking violently. "You think it was the FBI or a broker sending someone after you?"

"I don't know. But... I'm Italian, Shannon. I know how the mob works."

I rubbed my face as the confusion mounted. "The guy had an emblem on his gun. It was from an Italian family. Why the hell would the mob be after me?"

Shannon's eyes widened, but she didn't say anything. I wasn't sure if I wanted her to. My mind kept circling back to that gun, to the danger now surrounding me and her from every angle. The brokers, the FBI, and now this—someone with ties to the mob. Whoever they were, they were sending a message.

And it wasn't good.

I fell into a chair and stared at the chandelier above me, wondering if I had enough fight left in me to take them all down.

Shannon scurried off into the kitchen and returned with a steaming cup of coffee in hand, her robe cinched tightly around her body. She was as beautiful as the day I met her on the bus, and the distraction was well-needed. She placed the mug in front of me, and her brow furrowed as she glanced at the chaos of documents on the floor. It must have fallen out of my briefcase when I ran in.

"You're burning the midnight oil again?" she asked trying to sound casual but her voice trembled. I placed my hand on hers.

"Yeah, one of the new guys tonight is Stan Weinberg. He's sharp, knows the CME inside and out, and apparently has a reputation for making his opponents regret ever showing up."

Her eyes lit up with recognition. "Stan Weinberg? I've heard of him. That man's a bulldog in court. If anyone can help you bring down those brokers, it's him."

"That's good to hear," I replied cautiously. "But I don't want you getting involved, Shannon. Not after tonight. It's too dangerous."

She crossed her arms. "Michael, I'm already involved. Those brokers know who you are, and they sure as hell know where we live. For all we know that man that followed you could be outside our house right now." I glanced at the window but found no figure there and sighed in relief.

"My job is keeping you safe, not giving them another reason to come after us. Let me handle this."

Shannon's eyes softened, but the determination in her expression didn't waver. She sat slowly on my lap and caressed my face.

"Just promise me you'll be careful, Mike. You're not in this alone, even if you act like you are."

I squeezed her hand. "I promise. Now, go to bed. I've got this."

She hesitated for a moment before turning to leave. Her footsteps faded into the quiet of the house. I took a sip of the coffee she'd brought me, the bitterness cut through my exhaustion. The scattered papers stared back at me, a reminder that a battle was going on.

But the unease still lingered. My mind kept going back to the man I'd seen earlier, that figure in the fedora and trench coat.

Had I imagined him? Was I paranoid? Or had someone been following me for a reason?

Shannon had noticed it too, but she didn't think it was the mob. She knew me well enough to know I had no direct connections to them, just my Italian roots. It didn't make sense, and yet, the gunman's emblem had spoken a language I knew too well. A part of me wanted to dismiss it. But the part that had seen enough shady deals and under-the-table handshakes in my life couldn't shake the feeling that it was all connected.

I glanced back at the door as if expecting to see someone standing there, but the house was quiet. Shannon's voice echoed softly in my mind: *You're not in this alone.*

CHAPTER SIXTEEN

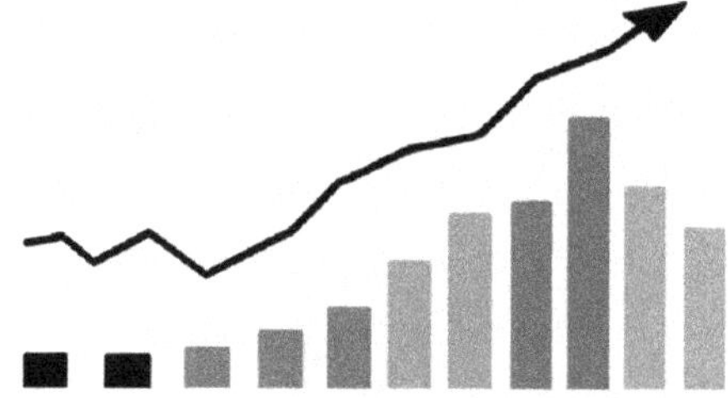

My body still ached from the previous night.

Dodging bullets wasn't exactly on my to-do list.

The events played on a loop in my head: the man in the trench coat, the gunfire, the sprint home through the alley. I hadn't slept much but the smell of coffee pulled me from bed. I shuffled toward the kitchen, expecting to find Shannon humming like she usually did in the mornings. Instead, she was sitting at the table, silent, staring at a piece of paper. Her face was pale, her fingers clutched the edges of the sheet tightly.

"Shan? What's wrong?" My voice was still rough from sleep.

She looked up at me, her eyes wide with a mixture of fear and anger. Wordlessly, she slid the paper across the table.

I picked it up and scanned each line.

Michael Russo,

Next time we won't miss, and now we know where your wife works and sleeps.

Anger surged through me as I read it again.

"Did this come in the mail?" I asked, sharper than I intended.

"Yes, I found it under the door this morning."

I read it again, folded the paper, and placed it carefully on the table.

Evidence.

"They're escalating," Shannon said. Her voice trembled but her expression was fearless.

That's why I love her.

"I'll handle it," I said firmly.

Her eyes flashed. "*We'll* handle it. Michael. They're threatening *us* now so whether you like it or not, I'm involved. "

I reached for her hand, and she let me take it. "But I will finish this. For you. For us."

She didn't say anything for a moment, just stared at me, searching for something in my expression. "Promise me you'll be careful?"

"I promise."

I SAT IN THE CONFERENCE ROOM AT THE CME, STARING AT THE polished wood of the table as the tension in the air thickened. Steve was tapping his pen against the edge of his notepad, Vince rocked on his chair nervously, and Brad looked like he was trying to bore a hole through the wall with his glare. Owen, ever calm, was flipping through a folder of evidence while Stan adjusted his tie, his expression unreadable. Across the table sat Mr. Reynolds, the CME's assistant compliance director, his face as stoic as the Chicago skyline.

Stan cleared his throat and slid a document across the table toward Reynolds. "This," he began, his tone measured but firm, "is a collection of trade anomalies that clearly indicate manipulation. Delayed trades, self-serving executions, front-running, patterns that can't be chalked up to coincidence."

Reynolds glanced at the document but didn't pick it up. "We appreciate your diligence, Mr. Weinberg. We'll investigate it."

Owen leaned forward, his voice laced with frustration. "You've been saying that for months, Reynolds. 'We'll investigate.' And yet, here we are—nothing's changed."

Reynolds folded his hands, his expression unchanging. "The CME takes all allegations seriously, but these things take time. We have protocols."

I felt the familiar churn of anger in my gut.

This wasn't just bureaucracy; it was stonewalling.

I took a deep breath, keeping my voice steady. "With all due respect, Mr. Reynolds, we're not here for more promises. We're here for action."

Reynolds met my gaze, his tone clipped. "And I'm telling you, Mr. Russo, action is being taken. These things aren't as simple as you might think."

Stan leaned on the table, a vein popped on his forehead out of frustration. "What's not simple is watching these brokers fleece the market while the CME condones these illegal activities . But there's a clause in your bylaws that could simplify things."

Reynolds arched a brow. "Oh?"

Stan tapped the table aggressively for emphasis. "Section 3.7If we gather enough signatures from independent traders, we can bring the issue to a vote in a specific pit. That's your rule, not ours."

The room went quiet for a moment. Even Reynolds seemed caught off guard.

"Assuming you can gather the signatures," Reynolds said finally, "you'd still need a majority vote. That's no small task."

"We know," I said, my tone unwavering. "But we're not here to play it safe. We're here to fix a broken system. *Your* broken system."

Brad, who'd been unusually quiet, spoke up. "We've got evidence, Reynolds. Real evidence. And more people joining us every day, so we'll get our signatures. You can't ignore this forever."

Reynolds stood and straightened his jacket. "As I said, we'll investigate. If you want to pursue this voting avenue, that's your prerogative. Now, if you'll excuse me, I have other important matters to attend to."

He walked out, leaving the room heavy with unresolved tension.

Owen broke the silence. "He's rattled."

"Good," Stan replied. "He should be. The clause is our best shot, and they know it."

Steve rubbed his temples. "Still, getting those signatures and securing a vote isn't going to be easy. Those brokers will fight us every step of the way."

"They already are," I said, the image of last night's attack flashing in my mind. But I kept that to myself. "We focus on the signatures. One step at a time."

Stan nodded. "Let's get started on that right away."

The group murmured in agreement, a flicker of cautious optimism in the air as we stepped out of the room and headed back to the pit. Brad and the others wasted no time, splitting off with clipboards in hand, already approaching traders for their signatures. As I watched them weave through the bustling floor, determination etched into their faces, a rare sense of hope stirred in me. We were finally on the verge of real change.

The pit buzzed with its usual chaos, but there was a tension in the air. The brokers moved carefully, their usual bravado tempered by the sight of the aqua blue-jacketed men hovering near the edges of the trading floor. It was quieter than normal, and the absence of held orders wasn't lost on anyone.

Owen was near the center of the pit, already yelling into the roar as he executed a quick trade. The moment he saw me, I motioned for him to follow and ducked into a corner near one of the terminals, just out of earshot of the others.

"What's up, Mike?" he asked softly.

I looked around before speaking.

"There was a guy last night," I said, flatly despite the adrenaline that still prickled under my skin. "He followed me home."

Owen stiffened. "What happened?"

"He pulled a gun," I said, swallowing hard as the memory surged back. "I managed to get away and I took a shortcut through the backyards." I paused and lowered my voice even further. "And then this morning, Shannon found a letter. A threat, Owen. They know where we live."

Owen let out a low whistle. "Christ, Mike. You should've called me last night. I'd have driven you home."

I forced a grim smile. "I didn't want to burden any of you. And anyway, I handled it."

"Yeah, well, you can't keep handling everything alone," he snapped. "And Shannon? Mike, she's in this whether you like it or not. What if they go after her next?"

The weight of his words hit me square in the chest. I'd been trying to protect her, but now it felt like my efforts were only painting a bigger target on her back.

"I'll figure it out," I said, but even I didn't believe the conviction in my voice.

"You better," Owen said, jabbing a finger at me. "Because if you don't, these bastards will. Let me drive you from now on, at least. No arguments, not until your car is back."

I nodded reluctantly, realizing I didn't have much of a choice anymore.

Just then, a murmur swept through the pit as traders began to notice something unusual. Orders were moving faster and cleaner. The brokers weren't holding them, not like they used to.

"You seeing this?" Owen said, scanning the activity around us.

"Yeah," I said, narrowing my eyes. "The rumors about the Feds have them spooked."

The brokers were subdued, their glances darting toward the blue jackets stationed near the exits. It was like watching predators circle, only this time, the brokers weren't the ones in charge. We made our way back to the pit. The tension in the S&P 500 was a living thing buzzing just under the surface, ready to snap. Traders crowded shoulder to shoulder, and the noise climbed higher and higher with each passing second. Somewhere to my left, a heavily accented voice cut through the din.

"Hey! That's the third time today you've front-run my orders, Donnelly!"

I turned toward the commotion just as one of the young traders involved in our coalition—Kevin—jabbed a finger at a broker in a green jacket, his face flushed with anger. Donnelly smirked and raised his hands in mock innocence.

"Relax, kid," Donnelly said, oozing condescension. "Maybe your orders just aren't fast enough."

"You think I don't see what you're doing?" Kevin snapped, his usual soft voice rising. "Holding my order until yours are filled? You're screwing all of us! I have evidence!"

The pit froze. It wasn't uncommon for accusations like this to fly, but shouting them in front of the entire floor, with the possibility of FBI agents watching from the gallery, was something else entirely.

Donnelly's smirk vanished. He stepped closer to Kevin, his voice low and threatening. "You better watch your mouth, kid, unless you want to find yourself on the wrong end of a bad trade."

Before anyone could react, Kevin shoved Donnelly hard in the chest. The broker stumbled back and suddenly all hell broke loose. Brokers and traders surged forward, shouting and jostling. Someone threw a punch, and the chaos spread like wildfire.

"Enough!" I shouted, pushing my way through the crowd. Owen was right behind me, his broad shoulders cutting a path as we reached the center of the fight.

It was worse than I thought. Kevin had a cut on his cheek and Donnelly was on the ground clutching his arm. Blood seeped through his sleeve.

"Jesus," Owen muttered, stepping in to pull Kevin back. "Who brought a knife into the goddamn pit?"

Donnelly groaned, his face pale as more traders circled around him.

"Somebody call an ambulance!" I yelled, scanning the floor.

The commotion was finally breaking apart when I noticed the blue jackets up in the gallery. They stood like statues, their eyes locked on the scene below. One of them, a tall man with sharp features, caught my gaze. For a moment, we stared at each other, and I felt a chill run down my spine.

He knew. He had to know how deep this went.

The sound of sirens broke the spell as paramedics arrived to take Donnelly away. Mr. Reynolds appeared moments later, flanked by a group of men in dark suits.

"Russo, McAuliffe, Patterson, Lawrence, Kaufman, Gadsen, Weinberg," Reynolds barked, his voice cut through the residual noise. "Conference room. Now."

Owen glanced at me, grimly. "Here we go."

I wiped the sweat from my brow.

What the fuck is happening now?

The conference room was a pressure cooker. I took a seat at the long table, surrounded by Owen, Stan, Dave, Will, and the others. On the opposite side, brokers sat with crossed arms and faces tight with suspicion and frustration. Mr. Reynolds was already at the head of the table, glaring down at the group as if trying to size us all up.

"You all know why we're here," Reynolds began, his voice sharp. "What happened on the floor today is unacceptable. We need to get to the bottom of it, and fast."

No one spoke but tension crackled in the air like static.

Finally, Dave's voice sliced through the silence. "This whole situation is out of hand. We've got the FBI here, apparently, and the violence is escalating—"

"They don't belong here!" one of the other brokers shouted. "This is our exchange, not some federal investigation playground! You've brought them in to ruin everything!" He pointed at me accusingly.

Before I could respond, Stan spoke up. "We didn't invite the FBI, and based on your reaction it's clear that they're here for guys like you."

His eyes flicked to me, and I knew what he was thinking. The threat I received wasn't far from the truth.

Owen added as if reading my mind. "And now we've got threats toward our family, physical intimidation, all because we dared to challenge the system that brokers corrupted. You want to talk about who invited who? Ask yourselves who's been pushing dual trading and the manipulation that comes with it." The room went dead quiet.

Dave's eyes narrowed. "We're talking about life and death here. Are we really going to pretend this isn't mob-related? Is that why the FBI's been breathing down our necks?"

The accusation hung in the air and the stranger's gun from last night flashed in my mind. And just like that, the room split. Brokers muttered among themselves while the traders on our side remained silent, watching the chaos unfold.

"Mob? Drug-related?" Will's voice was incredulous. "This isn't about that. This is about a system being bent to benefit a few at the cost of everyone else."

The argument escalated from there and voices rose as tempers flared. I could feel the weight of it all pressing on me. My thoughts kept circling back to the fight in the pit, to the knife, and to the threats against Shannon. I couldn't lose focus now. But damn, it was getting harder to hold everything together. Stan, who'd been quietly observing the chaos, finally slammed his hand on the table.

"Enough!" Stan barked and the room fell silent. He cleared his throat and faced Mr. Reynolds and the men surrounding him. "We're wasting time. Look, the only thing that matters right now is this: We need to stop dual trading. We've got the clause in the CME bylaws—if we can get enough signatures, we can force a vote."

A few traders looked at each other, eyebrows raised. They didn't need any more convincing.

Mr. Reynolds's gaze flicked to the brokers at the table, his eyes hard. "You're suggesting we vote to ban dual trading in the S&P pit? That's a bold move."

Stan didn't hesitate. "Yes, that's exactly what I'm suggesting. It's the only way to force the change we need."

The murmurs around the room grew louder. The brokers didn't like it. I could see it in their eyes, the way they shifted in their seats, and how they exchanged uncomfortable glances. The air was thick with resistance, but there was no denying that the idea was gaining traction. The traders were starting to look less like rebels and more like a movement, and the brokers knew it.

Reynolds held up a hand, silencing the room. "Fine. We'll vote. But you all know this isn't going to be easy. The brokers aren't just going to let this go."

Will Lawrence leaned forward, his voice low but firm. "If they're smart, they'll realize it's not just about them anymore. It's about the future of this exchange. The stakes are higher than anyone here wants to admit."

A broker across from him snorted. "This is ridiculous. You really think you can change something as fundamental as dual trading with a vote? You've lost your minds."

"We don't have the luxury of playing nice anymore," I snapped.

Mr. Reynolds looked at the men on either side of him before nodding slowly, his lips pursed tightly. "Then it's settled. We'll proceed with the vote."

CHAPTER SEVENTEEN

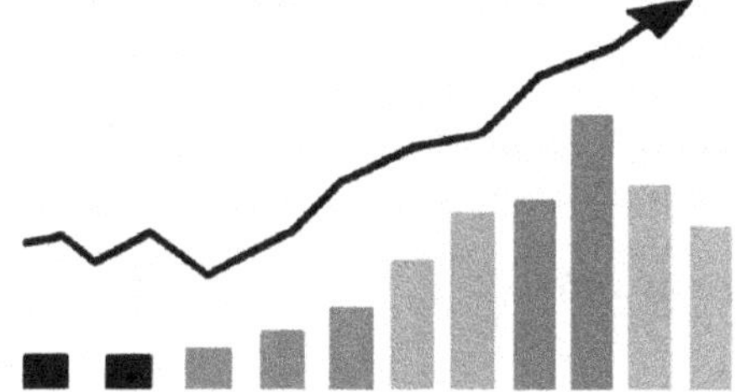

I stood near the back of the S&P pit, watching the frenzy of the last trades of the day. The noise, the shouting, the endless flipping of tickets, all the activity blurred together. The moment the bell rang, Owen stepped up onto a crate, calling for attention.

"Alright, everyone, quiet down!" His voice carried through the floor, and a few traders shot him annoyed looks, but it was all in good fun. Owen had a way of demanding attention without actually being serious about it.

"Come on, don't make me ask again!" Owen waved his arms, exaggerated enough that a few brokers stuck around, probably out of curiosity. Slowly, the noise died down, and the pit quieted to a dull hum. Some traders were still grumbling, but the energy had shifted.

Owen gave me a quick nod before calling out, "Mike! Get up here."

I made my way to the center of the pit, the space suddenly feeling a lot smaller as all eyes turned to me. A slight banter continued, familiar traders joked about Owen and me being too serious.

"Look at this guy, all business," Vince said with a grin, nudging Steve. "Mike's gonna bore us to death."

"Yeah, right," Steve chuckled. "We all know he's got a mean streak. What's he gonna do now, throw us in jail for talking too loud?"

Owen shot them a playful look but didn't say anything, just motioned for them to quiet down.

The chatter eventually faded. I could feel the shift in the room from lightheartedness to awareness. They weren't laughing now and even some of the brokers hung around. I looked at the familiar faces, all those who'd fought with me, and those who'd doubted me. They all waited.

I took a breath. "Alright," I said, loud enough to quiet the remnants of the banter. "Let's get down to business."

Owen motioned for silence, his face serious now.

"This," Owen said, "is where we start taking back control. Michael's got something to say."

I didn't look at any one person in particular as I started talking.

"Listen up," I began. "We're not here for the usual song and dance. We're here because it's time to act."

Murmurs spread across the room, but quickly hushed.

I cleared my throat. All eyes were on me now, and I wasn't about to let them down. I adjusted my stance as I tried to ignore the pounding in my chest and let my voice carry across the floor.

"My team and I have seen it all; dual trading in the S&P pit. Some of you are benefiting from it." I stared pointedly at the remaining brokers. "But it's a system that's choking the life out of this place. You all know it. Hell, you've probably been guilty of it yourself."

The murmurs began, and I could feel the tension. Some of the older traders, the ones who'd been in the game longer, exchanged glances, but they didn't interrupt.

I pressed on. "For those of you who don't know, dual trading is when brokers in the pit—people who are supposed to represent the interests of their clients—also trade on their own account. It's a conflict of interest, and it's been happening here for years."

I took a step forward, narrowing my gaze. "But we've got something now we didn't have before. Evidence. We've got the proof that they've been manipulating prices, gaming the system, and taking advantage of the very clients they're supposed to protect. That's why me and twenty-five of the most dedicated traders in this room—people who believe in this market—have been working to bring an end to it. We've got the backing, we've got the case, and we've been putting pressure on the CME. This isn't a theory anymore. This is real."

A few traders were nodding along, some shifted uncomfortably, and others looked skeptical.

"But here's the problem," I continued, "We can't take down the whole system right now. The CME isn't going to allow it, not with their biggest brokers pulling the strings. Not unless we go through the proper channels. They won't dismantle dual trading across the exchange, not with the people who benefit from it in power."

That stung, but it was the truth. We'd hoped—*hell, we thought*—maybe we could get a full-scale overhaul. But the CME was stubborn, and it wasn't going to happen. Not yet.

I clenched my jaw and scanned the pit. "But that doesn't mean we can't make a dent. I'm asking you to help us pass a vote to ban dual trading in the S&P pit. We may not have the whole exchange, but we can take this part of it down. The S&P pit's where it matters most. If we get the brokers out of the game here, that'll send a message."

The traders were listening intently, their expressions more serious now.

"Now, I know it's a big ask. Some of you might be worried about the fallout, but let me tell you, this is the only way forward. You want to change the game? Then vote. Take a stand. This isn't just about us. It's about the future of the S&P. We can be the ones to clean it up, and we can show the CME that we won't sit back and let them get away with this shit anymore."

There was a brief silence as my words hung in the air. Then, slowly, the murmurs started again, traders talking among themselves, weighing what I'd said. They weren't sure yet, but I could see the shift. A glimmer of hope, a spark of rebellion.

A trader near the front raised his hand. "So, you're telling us the CME's not going to just roll over for us, huh? We have to vote?"

"Exactly," I said, a bit sharper than I intended. "But if we come together on this, we can make it happen. And trust me, it'll be worth it."

I turned to look at the brokers who had stuck around to listen. They were quiet now, watching, not sure what to make of it. But I knew that they didn't like this. Not one bit. The tension in the pit was thick. It felt like something was about to break. But if I could get them to vote, to push through the ban on dual trading in the S&P pit, that would be a victory. A small one, but a victory.

I held their gaze for a long moment before speaking again. "So, I'm asking you, vote to take dual trading out of the S&P pit. If we can make that happen, we'll show the CME what real change looks like."

I could feel the weight of the question before it even came. The tension was still thick in the air, the pit quieter now, as the traders processed the idea I'd just laid out. I hadn't expected everyone to be on board right away, but I knew some of them would ask the tough questions. And I was ready for it.

One of the older traders, a guy I'd known for years, stepped forward. His face was creased with years of trading and navigating the chaos of the pit.

"So, Michael," he started, gruffly. "Why the hell are we only going after the S&P pit? Why not the whole exchange? Dual trading's everywhere."

The question hung there, sharp and direct. A few others in the pit nodded, agreeing with the sentiment. The truth was, I'd expected this one. I took a deep breath, trying not to let the frustration show. I'd been wrestling with this very issue for weeks, and now was the time to lay it out.

"Look." I stepped forward to meet his gaze. "You're right. Dual trading is a problem across the whole exchange, but the reality is we don't have the power to tackle the entire CME right now. Not with the way things are structured."

I let that sit for a moment, letting them all process the truth.

"The S&P pit, though," I continued, "That's a different story. It's one of the most important markets here. And it's been the biggest target for dual traders. Brokers are using it for their own gain. We've got a chance here, a real chance, to change it for the better. If we can get the vote in the S&P pit to pass, it'll send a message, not just to the CME, but to the entire exchange. It'll show that we're serious about fixing things."

I paused, letting the weight of the words sink in before continuing. "And yeah, it's a small victory in the grand scheme of things, but it's one that can snowball. If we take down dual trading here, other pits will follow. We'll have momentum. And when we've got the right evidence, when the pressure's on, we can take the fight to the rest of the exchange. But it starts here."

I saw the gears turning in his head. The rest of the traders were quiet now, watching, waiting for his reaction. He didn't respond right away, but I could tell he was thinking it over.

Finally, he nodded slowly. "I get it. We start here, make a stand, and then maybe we can take the rest down later."

Another trader, younger and with less experience, spoke up. "So, we're not going after the rest of the market yet because we don't have the support?"

"Exactly," I said, looking at him. "We need the right support for that, but if we can make a stand here it could be the catalyst for the bigger changes we need. We've got to win this battle first."

The older trader grunted in agreement, then threw a look at the other brokers in the pit. They were still quiet, but their eyes darted between each other, sizing up the situation.

"Alright, Russo," he said, "You've got my vote. Let's see if this works."

And with that, the first domino fell.

As the vote to ban dual trading in the S&P pit gained momentum, the brokers' retaliation shifted into overdrive. What had started as subtle threats—disguised as casual remarks—was now impossible to ignore. Whispers followed me through the hallways, veiled warnings disguised as "advice," and occasional glances exchanged between brokers that spoke volumes.

I could feel the tension in the air, thick like smoke. I had been targeted once, and now it seemed the whole floor was on edge. The rumors about the stabbing incident were spreading like wildfire with everyone talking about how close it had been and how violent things were getting. And my own personal attack—*well, that was just another piece of fuel to the fire.*

I overheard a trader say, "First it's a knife at work, now it's the family at home. What's next?"

Men on the floor were genuinely afraid for their lives. They were looking over their shoulders, questioning their own safety.

"Don't mess with the brokers, man. They'll take you out," someone muttered as I passed by.

I wanted to tell them to stand firm, to ignore the threats, but fear had already set in. I walked past another group of brokers, and one of them glared at me maliciously. The words "*next time*" echoed in my mind as I pushed through the crowd and made my way home.

I walked through the front door of my house and immediately sensed that something was wrong. Shannon stood in the living room with her back to the door. She stared out the window and her usual calm demeanor was gone.

"Shannon?" I asked, dropping my keys on the counter and running to her.

She turned slowly, revealing a pale face and wide tear-filled eyes.

"Michael," she croaked. "I... I don't know how to tell you this, but something happened today. A man came into my office."

Fear gripped me as I made her sit down and held her tightly. "Tell me what happened. Who was this man?"

"He was a new client. He came in for a meeting, just like any other day and any other client," she continued, her eyes unfocused, as if replaying the event in her mind. "But then... it wasn't just business anymore. He turned violent and tried to grab me. I... I don't know what happened, but I reached for the phone in time and security came. Not long after the police came and arrested him."

My blood ran cold. "Did he hurt you?"

"No, he just grabbed me a couple of times but I fought back."

Fuck.

I held on tighter to Shannon as she cried on my shoulder.

"What did he want?"

She pulled back and her hands trembled as she brushed a lock of hair from her face. "He didn't say much. Just... that you needed to stop. That if you didn't, things would get worse not just for you but for me as well."

The words hit me like a sledgehammer. It was clear that the brokers were getting desperate, trying to scare me into backing off. But threatening Shannon? That was crossing a line. After Shannon went to sleep, I immediately reached out to Owen and Stan. We needed to figure out who was behind this and who sent this guy to my family. I wasn't going to let this slide.

The next morning, we found ourselves at the local prison, waiting for the man to be brought in for questioning. He sat in a secure room there with his hands shackled to the table.

"Who sent you?" I demanded. I wasn't about to let this bastard off easy. "Who told you to attack my wife?"

He remained silent for a long moment, his eyes flicking to the guards standing nearby as if looking for a way out.

"You might think you're tough, but you're in deep. You attacked my wife, and there's nowhere to run. So, who paid you to do it?"

The man looked at me, his face twitching. Finally, after a long silence, he muttered, "Someone from the CME. I don't know who... just that they... they paid me."

I clenched my fists, but before I could press further, he added, "I can't say more. I won't say more."

Stan stood behind me, his face hard, but he didn't speak. We both knew there was nothing more we could get out of him. Whoever had ordered this attack was too careful to leave a trace. Someone at the CME wanted to send a message. We left the prison without any solid answers, but we knew the threats weren't going to stop there. They were escalating. Brad and Steve were violently attacked at a local bar, and Owen's family received letters similar to ours.

Days passed and the votes continued. The brokers were still playing their game of intimidation, trying to scare everyone back into submission, but the tide was shifting. The independents were starting to see the truth and as the end of the year loomed closer, I couldn't shake the feeling that the brokers were going to try something that would eventually force us to back down.

Can *we finish this fight, or* will *they crush us before we have* a *chance to see it through?*

CHAPTER EIGHTEEN

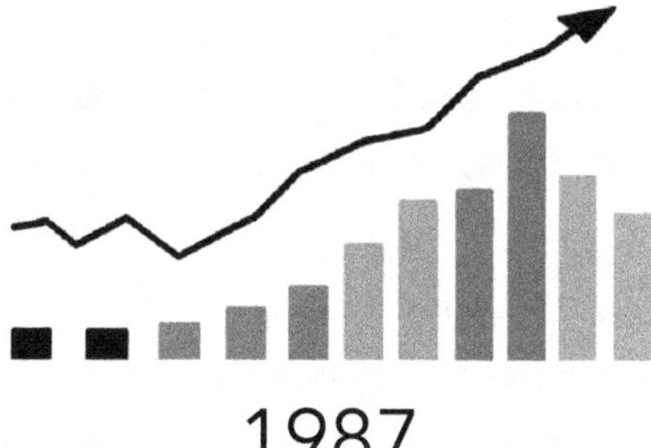

1987

The journalist arrived late, which wasn't a great start. I'd been watching the clock from my usual spot in the kitchen, sipping on coffee that had long gone cold. When the knock finally came, I opened the door to a man in his thirties clutching a notebook. His hair slightly was disheveled and he was surrounded by an air of impatience.

"Mr. Russo?" he asked, offering a quick handshake.

"That's me," I said. "Come in. Owen and Stan are waiting."

We sat at the dining table, the three of us traders facing off against the journalist like it was another fight in the pit. His name was Jeff something-or-other, and he didn't waste time diving into the questions.

"So, tell me about dual trading. Why is this such a big deal?" Jeff asked, his pen poised over the notebook.

I leaned forward, resting my elbows on the table. "Dual trading isn't just a conflict of interest—it's a loaded gun. Brokers use it to manipulate the market, trading on insider knowledge and screwing over the independent guys who don't have access to their order flow. It's dangerous, unethical, and it erodes the trust this exchange was built on."

Owen chimed in. "It's more than that. It's about integrity. Traders are walking away from the pits because they're sick of getting shafted. The CME's got rules, but dual trading makes a mockery of them."

Stan nodded, adding his own perspective. "What we're doing here, fighting to end it in the S&P pit, it's not just for us. It's for the future of this exchange. If the public can't trust the market, they'll stop investing. And when that happens, we all lose."

Jeff scribbled furiously, but I couldn't tell if he was impressed or just trying to keep up. "What kind of risks are you guys facing in pushing for this change?"

"Plenty," I said, my tone sharper than I intended. "Threats, intimidation, you name it. These brokers, they've got power, and they don't like us rocking the boat. But we're not backing down. This isn't about power for us, it's about doing what's right."

A week later, I sat in the same spot at the kitchen table, flipping through the pages of *The Chicago Tribune*. The article was buried in the business section, a half-page piece with a headline that read: **"Independent Traders Call for Change Amid Dual Trading Debate."**

It didn't take long to read, and it took even less time for my frustration to boil over. The piece was a watered-down version of the truth, full of vague language and missing the hard-hitting facts we'd laid out.

"Some independent traders," it read, *"have expressed concerns over dual trading practices, citing potential conflicts of interest. However, others argue that dual trading allows brokers to better manage risk and liquidity."*

I slammed the paper down.

"This was supposed to make waves, not ripple quietly into the background," I muttered.

Shannon sat across from me with a cup of tea and raised an eyebrow. "At least they didn't spin it against you, Michael."

"That's not the point," I snapped, though I immediately regretted the tone. "People need to know the truth, not some half-baked version of it. If we can't get the public on our side, what's stopping the brokers from keeping things the way they are?"

Shannon reached for my hand. "You've already made progress, Michael. Don't let one article derail you."

I stubbornly agreed with my wife, though the frustration simmered inside.

If the press won't *tell the whole story, we'll just have to make enough noise in the pits to force them to listen.*

The arbitration room buzzed with tension as everyone took their seats. The CME officials, brokers, independent traders, and Stan, who had taken up the role of our advocate, filled the space. The air was thick with unspoken rivalry, each faction eyeing the other with a mix of wariness and defiance.

Owen leaned toward me, muttering, "Feels like a showdown, doesn't it?"

I nodded. "Let's hope we don't leave this room with more bruises than answers."

Vince, seated to my left, adjusted his tie and murmured, "Bruises? If we lose this, we might as well kiss any future reforms goodbye."

Steve sat across the table and narrowed his eyes as he scanned the brokers. "They're too quiet. That's never a good sign."

Mr. Reynolds, flanked by other exchange officials, rapped his gavel on the table, signaling the meeting's start. "Gentlemen, we're here to finalize and review the results of the vote to ban dual trading in the S&P 500 futures pit. Let's maintain order and professionalism."

Stan wasted no time, standing to address the room. "Before we proceed, I'd like to reiterate why we're here. Dual trading isn't just an ethical gray area—it's a systemic problem. It allows brokers to exploit their position for personal gain, creating an uneven playing field that undermines trust in the market."

Dave sneered. "Spare us the sermon, Weinberg. Dual trading is how liquidity is maintained. You think banning it will improve things? You'll just dry up the market."

Brad shot back, his gruff voice cut through the room. "Liquidity? Don't insult our intelligence, Dave. We all know this isn't about market health—it's about padding your pockets while the rest of us take the hits."

Reynolds held up a hand, calling for calm. "Let's stay focused. The arguments have been heard. The votes have been cast. This meeting is about determining the results."

Stan's voice was steady but firm. "With all due respect, Mr. Reynolds, we've heard this rhetoric before. What we're asking for isn't radical—it's reform. If the CME doesn't take action to regulate dual trading, it risks losing credibility. That's not a threat; it's a reality."

Will, seated with the brokers, folded his arms and spoke up. "You all think you're above the system, but the vote will show otherwise. The majority wants fairness, not favoritism."

Reynolds exchanged a glance with the officials beside him, his expression unreadable. "We'll get to the results. First, I want to address the allegations of intimidation surrounding this vote."

Owen stood. "Intimidation? That's rich coming from the brokers. My colleagues and I have been on the receiving end of threats for weeks—threats involving our families, aimed at silencing us and scaring others from voting."

Dave scoffed. "Baseless accusations."

Stan didn't miss a beat. "Baseless? We have multiple witnesses who can attest to brokers pressuring traders, spreading rumors, and even resorting to physical intimidation. If the CME values transparency, it'll acknowledge these tactics for what they are: an attempt to manipulate the outcome."

The room fell into a tense silence as Stan's words echoed in the small space. I cleared my throat and looked at each man on the panel.

"It's time the CME decides whose side it's on: fairness or corruption."

Reynolds became clearly uncomfortable and responded, "The CME takes these allegations seriously, Mr. Russo. However, the integrity of the voting process remains intact. Now, let's move forward."

An official handed Reynolds a sealed envelope. He opened it slowly and the room held its collective breath. I heard my heartbeat in my ears, every second dragged out like an eternity. I glanced at Owen, who was gripping the edge of the table, and Brad, whose jaw was set in determination. Vince drummed his fingers on the table, the only sign of his nerves, and I was too afraid to look at Steve.

Reynolds finally looked up, but his expression gave nothing away. "The results are in."

Everyone went completely still. Reynolds let the silence hang for a moment, heightening the tension in the room.

Then, with a slight cough, he announced, "The motion to ban dual trading in the S&P 500 futures pit has passed."

The room erupted in a mix of reactions. Independent traders clapped and cheered, the tension that had gripped us finally breaking into palpable relief. On the other side of the room, the brokers sat in stunned silence, their smug confidence wiped clean.

Owen slapped the table and grinned. "That's it! We fucking did it!"

Stan, ever the composed lawyer, allowed himself a small smile. "This is a moment to savor. A win like this doesn't come easy."

I turned to them, my chest swelled with a mix of pride and disbelief. "We did it. They can't ignore us anymore."

A booming laugh came from Vince, who clapped me on the back. "Damn right, Russo. About time someone leveled the playing field."

Steve chimed in, his voice full of satisfaction. "The independent traders aren't just background noise anymore."

Reynolds raised his hand for quiet. "Gentlemen, let me remind you—this is a victory, but it comes with responsibility. The CME expects you all to abide by the new regulations and prove this change was worth it."

"Trust us," Stan said, sharply, "we'll show you it was the right move. The S&P pit will thrive without dual trading, and maybe the rest of the exchange can follow suit."

Reynolds gave a curt nod before standing to leave with the other officials. The brokers, still fuming, followed suit, muttering curses under their breath.

As we filed out of the arbitration room, Brad grabbed my shoulder. "You know this isn't the end, right? They'll try to fight back in other ways."

"Let them," I said, my voice steely. "We've shown we're not afraid to take them on."

By the time we returned to the trading floor, word of the vote had spread and we caught sight of a few independent traders celebrating in their own ways on the floor.

Stan leaned toward me, a rare grin lighting up his face. "This is just the start, Michael. But damn, it feels good."

Owen, ever the optimist, laughed. "Drinks are on me tonight. Let's celebrate this one."

As I looked around at the jubilant faces of my fellow traders, I allowed myself a moment of satisfaction. We'd fought like hell, and for once, we'd won.

THE BAR BUZZED WITH THE KIND OF ENERGY ONLY A HARD-FOUGHT victory could create. Owen raised his glass high, his face flushed from a mix of adrenaline and whiskey.

"To us! To every damned independent trader who refused to back down!"

A chorus of cheers followed as glasses clinked together in messy synchrony.

Stan, leaning against the bar, smirked. "Careful, Owen. You keep toasting like that, and I'll be carrying *you* home."

"Let him have his moment," I said, grinning. "He earned it. We all did."

As the night went on, the stories started to flow, each trader taking turns recounting their own piece of the battle.

Vince, seated at a corner table nursing a scotch, waved me over. "Russo," he called.

I grabbed my beer and made my way to him.

"Hell of a thing we pulled off," I said, sliding into the chair across from him.

He nodded, swirling his drink. "It's not every day the little guys win. You should be proud of what you did."

"Thanks, Vince. Means a lot coming from you."

He leaned forward, his eyes narrowing like he was about to impart some great secret. "Now, let me give you a piece of Chicago wisdom. You ever get pulled over for speeding?"

I chuckled, caught off guard. "Not recently, why?"

"Well," he said, lowering his voice, "if you do, don't try to bribe the cop outright. Stick fifty bucks on the dashboard and tell him it's for lunch. Nine times out of ten, you'll drive away without a ticket."

I laughed, shaking my head. "Is that so?"

"Trust me," he said with a wink, "it's an art."

Owen joined us, dropping into a chair with another round of drinks. "What's so funny over here?"

"Vince is giving me tips on dealing with Chicago cops," I said.

Owen grinned. "Oh, you mean the fifty-buck lunch trick? Classic Vince."

The three of us sat and shared more stories. Soaking in the camaraderie of the moment. By the time the bartender called for last orders, the bar was still alive with energy. I stood up, raising my glass one last time.

"To all of us. This isn't just a win for the S&P pit—it's a win for what's right."

A roar of approval echoed through the room as glasses went up.

The streets of Chicago were unusually quiet as I drove home. The adrenaline from the night hadn't worn off, and I found myself replaying the scenes from the bar in my mind. I was just a few blocks away from hitting the highway when I saw the dreaded flash of blue and red lights in my rearview mirror. My heart sank.

"You've got to be kidding me," I muttered under my breath, easing the car to the side of the road.

The officer approached slowly, his flashlight cutting through the night as it swept over the back of my car. I rolled down my window, trying to keep my expression calm, though my mind raced.

"Evening, sir," the cop said, his voice steady. "You know why I pulled you over?"

"Honestly, Officer, I don't," I said, hoping to sound sincere.

"You were doing 45 in a 30," he replied, tilting his head toward the speed limit sign a few yards back.

Great, of all the nights I forgot to watch my speed.

Then Vince's words came back to me, as clear as if he were sitting in the passenger seat. *Stick fifty bucks on the dashboard and tell him it's for lunch.*

I hesitated for a moment, debating whether or not to actually go through with it. But the thought of a speeding ticket, and the inevitable lecture from Shannon, made the decision for me.

I reached into my wallet, pulled out a crisp fifty-dollar bill, and placed it on the dashboard.

"Officer," I said, doing my best to keep a straight face, "how about I buy you lunch instead of paying for a ticket?"

The cop froze, his flashlight lingering on my face for a beat longer than I was comfortable with. His expression was unreadable, and I braced myself for what was about to come next.

Then, to my utter disbelief, he chuckled.

“Lunch, huh?” he said, his lips curling into a grin. “That’s a new one.”

I shrugged, trying to play it cool. “Figured it was worth a shot. A guy at the bar tonight swore it works every time.”

The officer was clearly amused. “You’ve got some guts, I’ll give you that. Tell you what. I’ll let you off with a warning this time. But keep your speed down, yeah? Next time, no amount of lunch money is going to help you.”

“Understood Officer,” I said, the relief washing over me.

He gave the roof of my car a light tap. “Drive safe.”

As he walked back to his patrol car, I couldn’t help but laugh to myself.

“Damn it, Vince.” I chuckled to myself. “You were fucking right.”

CHAPTER NINETEEN

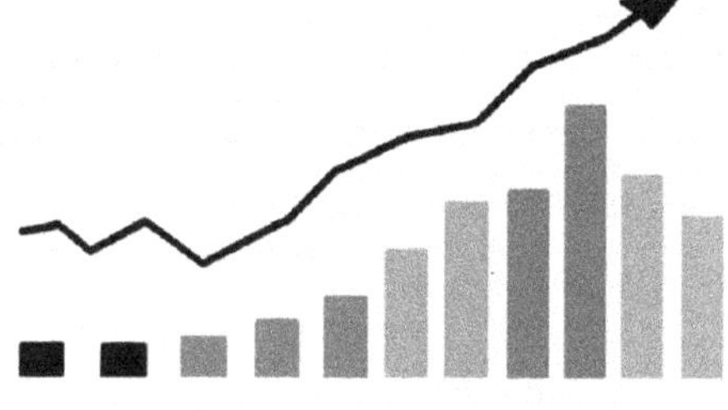

May 1987

A month had passed since the announcement, and the atmosphere on the CME floor had shifted. The euphoria from the ban on dual trading had faded, replaced by a tension that buzzed in the air like static before a storm. The brokers, once confident in their dominance, were visibly on edge. Their quiet, seething resentment was impossible to ignore, and their eyes lingered on us longer than before.

I stood at the edge of the pit again, watching the frenetic action unfold as orders were shouted across the floor. Owen was by my side, scanning the room for any signs of trouble.

"They're not exactly welcoming us with open arms, are they?" Owen muttered, eyeing a group of brokers who were whispering to each other in the corner. "Think we're in for a rough ride today?"

"Doesn't feel like it's over yet," I replied, tightly. "But we knew this wasn't going to be easy. We've made enemies, Owen. And the brokers don't forget easily."

Just then, Vince walked by, his usual confidence absent. He was a bit more tense these days, his posture stiffer, like he was constantly bracing for the next hit.

"You all right man?" I asked him, eyeing his rigid frame.

Vince stopped and flashed me a weary smile. "Just keeping my head down," he said, though his eyes betrayed the strain. "The fallout's starting to come in. They've been sending messages, trying to intimidate the traders. Some threats. Some more... creative methods."

"Creative methods?" Owen asked, raising an eyebrow.

Vince gave a small, almost humorless laugh. "Let's just say I'm getting more attention than I care for. One of the brokers sent a 'gift' to one of the traders in our coalition—some... fishy business going on. But we're still standing."

Owen looked at me, concern flickering in his eyes. "You think it's going to escalate?"

"Already has," I muttered. "They'll find a way to make us pay. I mean the bastards almost got me killed."

The group of brokers who had been talking earlier was now watching us, and I could feel their eyes boring into the back of my neck. Dave was amongst them, and he broke away from the huddle and strode over to us.

"Congrats, Mikey," he said mockingly. "You really showed us, didn't you? Ban dual trading and save the day."

"I didn't save anything. I just made it a little harder for you to cheat, Dave."

He glared at me. "Harder? We'll see. You've started a wave that's going to crash down on all of you sooner or later. You've disrupted the natural order."

I stepped toward him, feeling the heat rise in my chest. "Natural order? You mean the one where a few people get to stack the deck while the rest of us get screwed?"

Dave sneered. “You’ll learn, Russo. The brokers run the show here. And when you try to shake things up, you better be ready for the consequences.”

Vince shook his head. “We’re not backing down. You want to play dirty? Go ahead. But don’t pretend like we haven’t seen it all before.”

Dave looked like he was about to say something else, but he held back. With a final, cold look, he turned and walked away, his heel tapping against the floor with each step.

Owen glanced at me. “You think that’s the worst of it?”

“Not even close,” I replied, my mind racing. “They’ve just started playing their hand. And we’re going to be in the middle of it.”

The tension didn’t ease after that encounter. If anything, it felt like we were waiting for a storm that was bound to hit, and the calm before it only made the anxiety sharper.

The brokers didn’t waste any time rallying together. It wasn’t just the veiled threats anymore—things were escalating. I’d walk across the floor and hear murmurs of “watch your back.” Even small things started to feel off. A trade ticket with a number that didn’t match what I had in mind.. It was like someone was watching for any opportunity to make us look incompetent.

I could tell Owen was feeling it too. He was usually one to shrug off a bad trade or a few harsh words, but lately, he seemed more on edge.

“I’m getting all kinds of weird looks today,” Owen muttered during a break. “The kind that don’t come with a smile.”

“I’ve noticed,” I replied, my voice low. “It’s not just looks, though. They’re trying to get under our skin and sabotage us any way they can. We have to keep our heads on straight.”

Then, there were the rumors. They spread like wildfire, as they always did in this environment. We heard whispers that I was only in this fight for personal gain, that I was using the S&P reform to push my own agenda. Some of the brokers even said Owen and I were being manipulated, that we didn’t realize we were just pawns in a larger game. The worst part? A lot of traders on the floor started to believe it. Not everyone, but enough to make me realize how fragile this coalition was. A few well-timed whispers could tear everything apart.

At one point, I even overheard one of the CME officials muttering to a colleague, "This whole thing is becoming a circus. They've stirred up more unrest than we needed. Who do they think they are, making waves like this? It's disrupting the whole floor."

It felt like a slap in the face. For months, we had fought tooth and nail for fairness against corrupt practices and this was how the officials responded? By blaming us for the unrest we'd caused by demanding change? It made me feel like we were the ones in the wrong, as if we were the problem rather than the brokers who'd been exploiting the system for their own gain.

Owen caught the exchange, his expression hardening. "Did they just blame us for all this? For trying to fix a broken system?"

"Seems like it," I muttered. "Guess they'd rather we stayed in the shadows, letting the brokers do whatever they want."

I could feel the weight of their disdain, and every inch of me wanted to snap back. But I knew better than to let it show. If we gave in to the pressure, if we showed even a hint of weakness, they'd pounce.

Stan, our lawyer, had warned us this would happen. "They'll blame you for the disruption, even if you're the ones trying to fix it. They'll look for any excuse to discredit you. You just need to keep pushing forward, no matter what."

It wasn't easy. The threats, the rumors, the sabotage—it all chipped away at us. But with every new obstacle, we had one thing going for us: unity. The coalition was still standing, still fighting. And as the pressure built, I reminded myself of one thing: this wasn't just about us anymore. It was about the entire floor, the integrity of the market, and whether we were going to let the brokers keep running the show.

So, I kept my eyes forward, kept my voice steady, and pushed back the fear that gnawed at the edges of my mind. They could threaten us, intimidate us, and make our lives difficult, but they could never change what we accomplished.

The following days felt like a constant barrage. Every time I turned around, it seemed like the brokers were one step ahead, finding new ways to chip away at us.

It started with a letter.

It was simple and nothing flashy. Just a plain envelope with no return address. I opened it in the quiet of my office, my fingers trembled more from anticipation than fear.

"They're watching you," the letter read, scrawled in jagged handwriting.

That was it. No explanation, no threats, just those three words that hung in the air like a warning. The floor felt colder as I read it again. If someone was truly watching me then I couldn't show weakness. I'd come this far, and I couldn't let a few words on paper stop me. I crumpled the letter and tossed it into the trash, but the unease lingered at the back of my neck.

Later that evening, I ran into Owen at the local bar, trying to drink away the stress. I sat down beside him and felt my heart sink as he told me what had happened to his car.

"Someone keyed it," Owen said quietly, his hands clenching around his drink. "And they slashed the tires. Right outside my house."

I could hear the fury in his voice but he wasn't just angry; he was worried too.

"Any idea who did it?" I asked, though I already knew the answer.

"I don't need to know. I can feel that it's them. They're trying to scare me into backing off. Trying to make me second-guess this whole fight."

"Don't let them get in your head," I replied.

"Yeah, but I keep thinking 'What if my mother was in the car, or my sister,' you know?"

"I know..."

In the back of my mind, fear crept in as I thought about the man who was sent to Shannon's office. This wasn't just about the trade pit anymore. This was personal. The brokers weren't just trying to protect their territory, they were coming after us, trying to break us through our family and personal life.

It wasn't long before I heard more rumors. Brad caught wind of some brokers talking in hushed voices, their words dripping with malice.

"They're not just targeting us," Brad said when we met later that night. "They're talking about making life hell for anyone supporting the reform. They're willing to do whatever it takes to crush us, even if it means hurting our loved ones."

I thought about Shannon and tried to push away all the potential bad things that they could do to her, but it was always there, lurking around in the shadows of my mind. Every morning, I could see the strain in her eyes and the worry etched into her face and I couldn't help but wonder if this had all gone too far. I knew I was risking more than just my career now. I was putting my wife in danger.

"What do you suggest we do, huh Mike?" Brad's voice pulled me back to reality.

I thought for a second before answering. "Let's regroup."

The traders sat in a circle, some nursing drinks, others tapping nervously on the table. Owen, Stan, and I had gathered the group to remind everyone that we weren't in this alone. But as the meeting wore on, it became clear just how deep the intimidation ran.

Steve was the first to speak up. His voice was strained, betraying the pain he'd been hiding. "You guys have no idea what this has cost me," he began, looking around the room at the familiar faces of those who had fought alongside him. "The day those photos were leaked, my wife got a copy delivered to her." He paused, swallowing hard, his eyes distant for a moment as he relived the memory. "She thought I was involved in something dirty. Something shady. I almost lost her. I spent days convincing her it was all a lie, that it was just a damn photo."

There was a murmur around the table as the weight of Steve's words sank in. Vince leaned forward, his brow furrowed. "So, that's why you've been off the grid these last few weeks?"

Steve nodded slowly. "Yeah. I had to fix things at home before I could even think about fighting back. It's not just us. It's our families too."

The silence that followed was heavy as each man reflected on the toll the battle had taken on their personal lives. I decided to tell them about my incident.

"I get it, Steve," I said, leaning forward and looking at each of the men around the table. "But you haven't heard the worst of it." I could see the curiosity building in their eyes, the anticipation of the story they hadn't heard before. "A few nights ago, I was followed home. Some guy was tailing me through the city. I didn't realize it until I got onto the train and he sat a few seats away from me. Next thing I knew he was shooting at me before I could leave the train. I somehow got out safely, but I had no gun so I ran. I ran out of the train and into my house where I grabbed my gun, but he was gone."

A low murmur of disbelief rippled through the room. Brad's face went pale. "What the hell? Why didn't you tell us sooner, Mike?"

I looked at him and shrugged. "Owen and Stan knew about it. I didn't think much of it at first. But then not long after that, someone showed up at Shannon's office. She had a client meeting, and the guy got violent. He attacked her before security stepped in. The police arrested him, but he wouldn't say who sent him. Just said someone from the CME told him to 'take care of' Shannon and me."

The room went completely silent, every face locked in a mix of shock and anger. Stan's fist clenched as he remembered the visit to the police station. "That was crossing the line, Michael. That was... just too fucked up and personal."

"It is," I said. "It's not just about us anymore. It's about our families. And they're trying to break us. But we can't let them. I suggest that you guys invest in a weapon, for self-defense, just in case push comes to shove."

Owen, who had been quietly processing the information, spoke up steadily. "They've made it personal, and that just means we fight harder."

Stan looked around the room, his voice firm. "We have to keep pushing. No matter what they throw at us. We've made history, and we can't let them rewrite it."

"Well, if it is the FBI who's been showing up in those blue jackets," he said, and everyone's eyes shifted to him, "then hopefully all these things will be reported and come to an end. They'll have to investigate the intimidation and every damn thing that's happened to us."

The room went quiet once more as our thoughts turned toward the men in blue jackets.

"I guess we'll see how far this thing goes," Vince added with a small smile.

It was then that I realized what we had risked. It wasn't just our careers on the line but our lives and families too. I looked around the room at the men who had stood by us and a deep sense of respect for them washed over me. All twenty-five of them had stepped up, knowing the cost, knowing the dangers, and still, they fought with us. They didn't back down, and neither did we. As the reality of what we had endured settled in, I couldn't help but hope that one day all the injustices we'd faced would be recognized and the wrongs committed against us would be righted. And I prayed that the men in blue jackets were truly there to protect the integrity of the CME.

CHAPTER TWENTY

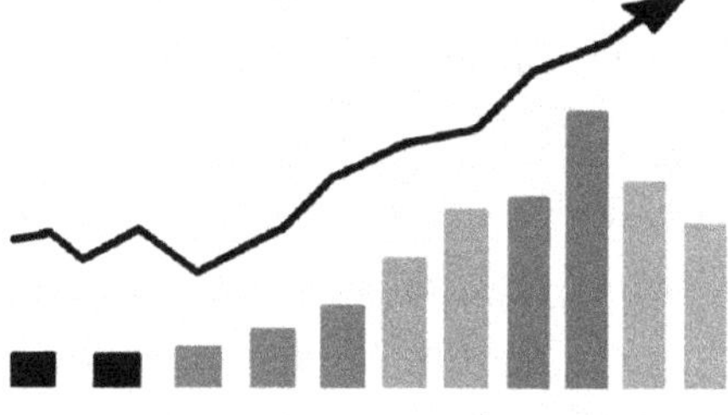

October 1987

"Get ready, it's gonna get ugly," Owen said, his voice barely audible over the growing roar of the CME floor.

I didn't need him to tell me. I could see it myself. The S&P 500 futures were plummeting, the ticker flashing red as if it was trying to warn us all. Brokers were barking orders, moving faster than I had ever seen them, their faces set in grim determination. But it wasn't working. Panic had already begun to seep through the cracks.

I glanced around the pit, my eyes locking with Stan's. He was working his trades, as usual, but the tension was different today. The air was almost suffocating, as if the weight of the market's collapse was pressing down on all of us. We had been here before, during the smaller crashes and dips, but nothing like this. The numbers on my monitor were changing faster than I could track. The market was unraveling in front of my eyes. Each drop felt like a punch to the gut, but I couldn't look away.

Owen elbowed me again, this time with urgency. "Michael, the market's crashing, but it's not just that. The FBI's here. I knew that was them!"

I turned to him, the weight of his words sinking in. "The FBI?" My voice shook a bit, betraying the panic I was trying to keep hidden.

"Yeah," Owen said. "The investigation's only just beginning, but the agents are everywhere. We've been exposed."

Just then, a man approached the group and flashed his badge with a cold, professional stare. "Agent Blackwell, FBI," he said, his voice clipped. "We're here investigating potential federal violations related to trading practices. You'll all need to cooperate while we conduct our work."

"Yes, sir." We responded in unison.

It took a moment for everything to sink in. The FBI sniffing around the CME for weeks before the coalition had pushed to ban dual trading in the S&P pit was just a rumor at first. But this was different. The market's freefall had just confirmed what we'd all feared. This was the catalyst for something much bigger than any of us had anticipated.

I took a deep breath and glanced at the brokers who, despite their frantic activity, were trying to maintain some semblance of control. There was no hiding from the truth now. We'd fought for years to eliminate dual trading, but even that victory seemed small against the enormity of what was unfolding.

The crash, the FBI investigation, the systemic rot—it was all coming to a head. My hands gripped the edge of the trading post, and I couldn't help but think about how much had changed in such a short time.

"Watch yourself, Michael," Stan said, walking past me. He didn't need to explain. The tension in his voice said it all. As the numbers on the screen continued their downward spiral, I couldn't help but feel a cold, heaviness settle over me. The world was about to change, and we were in the thick of it. The reform we'd fought for was more important than ever, but I wasn't sure any of us knew what was going to happen next.

The roar of the pit grew louder with the familiar chaos as traders shouted, but this time their voices were cracking with panic. I turned to Owen, who was scanning the floor, his eyes darting from one corner to another. I knew what he was looking for.

The FBI agents.

They had slipped in quietly every day, wearing those aqua blue jackets that caught everyone's attention. It was no surprise that the feds were here to dig deep into the CME. I caught a glimpse of one agent standing near the back of the pit, speaking with a broker who seemed to be trying to explain something, but his voice shook. Another agent was chatting with an exchange official who looked like he was about to break out in a cold sweat. The agents' eyes were sharp and calculating. They weren't here to watch the market crash; they were here to dissect the rot underneath it.

Owen yelled from his place. "They're everywhere, Michael! They were watching."

My throat was dry as the reality set in. I was sure that they'd been investigating dual trading for months before us. But this was different from the dual trading. There was something more to the CME than we'd ever known, something darker lurking beneath the surface. The feds were here to uncover the deeper rot, the hidden corruption that had been festering for years. And they weren't leaving until they dug it all out.

Stan walked over and pulled Owen and me aside. "You both see them?" he asked quietly, nudging toward the floor.

"Yeah," I replied. "Looks like they're making their move."

"Their move?" Stan asked, frowning. "Michael, I don't think they're here to play. This is bigger than the dual trading ban. They've got eyes on everything, corruption, manipulation, the whole damn exchange."

Owen clenched his jaw. "They're gonna burn the whole thing down, aren't they?"

Stan didn't answer right away, but his expression said it all. "We don't know how far they'll go. But we're in the middle of it now."

As the market continued its descent into chaos, the FBI was methodically moving through the crowd, their presence a quiet but undeniable force. The agents weren't just looking for the smaller infractions, the petty corruption we had dealt with on the floor. No, they were going after the root of the problem.

I glanced back toward the brokers, who had fallen silent. The usual banter and murmurs were gone, replaced by a quiet tension that hung in the air. They were watching the feds with a nervous energy that wasn't lost on me. I could feel the unease ripple through the room, an undercurrent that was hard to ignore.

Owen leaned in, his voice barely above a whisper. "They're not just here for the dual trading, are they?"

I shook my head, eyes fixed on the agents moving through the crowd. "No, this is bigger. They're looking for something deeper. Something the exchange has been hiding for a long time."

"Michael," Owen said softly, pulling me from my thoughts. "This is it, isn't it? The end of the line for them."

I took a deep breath. I didn't know how this would play out, but I knew one thing for sure: the fight wasn't over. In fact, it was only just beginning. The FBI might have come for the CME, but we had already done something they hadn't counted on—we had started the reforms that would make it harder for the brokers to hide.

"We've come this far," I said, my voice steady despite the uncertainty. "We can't back down now. They may be watching us, but they don't know what we've already done."

Stan gave me a curt nod. "We stay the course. We've changed things, Michael. We've made history. Now, let's make sure we don't let it all unravel."

Stan, Owen, and I sat in the small, sterile room, the door shut tight behind us. The tension hung thick in the air, like we were all holding our breath. The FBI agents had called us in for what was supposed to be a confidential meeting, and the severity of the situation was not lost on any of us. Agent Blackwell stood at the front of the room, his arms crossed, a stern look on his face. He was flanked by two other agents, both looking just as grim. The walls seemed to close in as the weight of the moment settled over us.

"Gentlemen," Blackwell started, his voice as heavy as him, "we're here to talk about the Chicago Mercantile Exchange and its failure to regulate dual trading." He paused, letting the words land with the weight they deserved. "We've been investigating the CME for months now. What we've uncovered is nothing short of systemic corruption."

My stomach twisted as he spoke, but I forced myself to keep still, my gaze fixed on the floor. Owen shifted uncomfortably beside me, but Stan, ever the professional, gave a barely perceptible nod.

Blackwell continued, "Brokers, who should've been acting as market facilitators, have been using their dual roles—both as traders and as brokers—to manipulate the system for personal gain. These actions have caused widespread damage, undermining the integrity of the entire exchange."

This was the nightmare we'd feared, but it was happening. The very exchange I'd spent my career trying to protect, the one I'd fought for, was being torn apart by the very people who were supposed to uphold it.

Blackwell continued, "The CME's negligence allowed this to flourish. They didn't enforce the necessary safeguards to stop dual trading. As a result, countless customers and traders have been exploited, and the market has been manipulated."

Owen's hands clenched into fists at his sides. "So, what now?" he asked, his voice low but laced with anger. "What happens to all of us who've been playing by the rules?"

"That's where it gets complicated," Agent Blackwell said, his eyes narrowing. "We're about to move forward with federal indictments. Several high-ranking officials, including brokers, have been identified as part of the conspiracy. The CME's corruption is about to be exposed to the world, and we expect significant fallout."

I felt a cold shiver run down my spine. "And what does that mean for the independent traders?" I asked, my voice barely above a whisper.

Blackwell paused, and for the first time, his demeanor softened. "You'll be caught up in this, too. It's inevitable. The systemic failures run deep, and the truth is going to come out—whether you're ready for it or not. But know this: without your efforts, the reform would never have happened. The fact that dual trading has been banned is the only thing that has stopped this from being even worse."

Stan exhaled slowly, as if processing the magnitude of what was unfolding. "So, the feds are going after the brokers—and the CME itself?"

"Yes," Blackwell confirmed, his gaze sharp. "We'll be issuing indictments soon. The collapse of the exchange is coming, but the damage has already been done. The public will know everything. Every scandal, every deal, every piece of corruption."

The weight of his words hung in the air like a suffocating fog. The truth was finally coming to light. The very system that had kept this corruption hidden for so long was about to be exposed. And the brokers? They were about to pay for it.

I could feel the relief inside me that justice was finally coming. But it was mixed with an undeniable fear. The CME, as we knew it, was on the brink of collapse. Our victory in banning dual trading had been important, but now the entire structure we'd worked to protect was going down in flames.

I looked at Stan, his jaw set and his eyes unwavering. He had been my rock through this entire process. "So, what now?" I asked, the question hanging in the room like the proverbial elephant.

"We brace ourselves," Stan said, his voice steady, but there was a hint of something deeper in his tone. "We've done the right thing. We exposed the truth. And now, we deal with the consequences. We've made history, Michael. Whether we like it or not, history is unfolding right before our eyes."

The agents stood up, signaling the end of the meeting. As I left the room, my mind was racing. The truth was finally coming out. The exchange would never be the same, and neither would we. But at least, for the first time, we had a chance to truly change things.

As I walked out into the hall, Owen caught my arm, his face a mix of apprehension and resolve. "We're in this together, right?" he asked, his voice firm.

"Always," I replied, my mind focused on the battle ahead.

We had fought for the truth, and now, we were going to watch it tear down the walls that had kept it hidden for so long. And when the dust settled, I hoped the world would see it for what it truly was: a victory for the traders and a defeat for those who had profited off corruption.

We stood in the hallway, the weight of the meeting heavy on our shoulders. The agents had left us with a sense of finality, their departure leaving a silence that felt as if the world was holding its breath. But despite the severity of the situation, despite the looming fallout of the FBI's investigation and the systemic collapse of the CME, a quiet resolve settled over me.

Owen's voice broke the silence first. "We've done it, Michael. It may not feel like a win right now, but it is. Dual trading's gone. They can't undo that."

I nodded as I stared at the ground, my mind still reeling from the implications of what we'd just heard. The collapse of the CME, the indictments, the exposure of corruption—it was all overwhelming. But Owen was right. In the midst of all this chaos, there was something we could hold on to: the reform we'd fought for had shielded the market. The ban on dual trading was in place, and that was something no one could take away.

I glanced over at Stan, who had been unusually quiet. He met my gaze and offered a small, approving nod. "We've been through hell to get here," he said, his voice low and steady. "But we held the line. We fought for something bigger than all of us."

"It's bigger than just the S&P pit," I replied, the words slipping out before I could stop them. "This was about changing how this entire industry works. It was about exposing the rot in the system and pushing for something real, something lasting."

Owen stepped closer, his hand resting on my shoulder. "And that's exactly what we've done. You've been carrying this weight, Michael, but we're all in this together. We've got each other's backs."

His words were like a lifeline, grounding me in the storm of emotions swirling inside. The relief, the fear, the uncertainty—it was all there, mixing into something I wasn't sure I could fully understand just yet. But one thing was certain: we'd made history. And that was something I could hold on to.

The sound of footsteps broke our quiet moment. It was Brad, looking as worn out as the rest of us. "I just got a call from a source," he said, his face grim. "The feds are tightening their grip. They're coming for everyone."

We'd preserved the integrity of the market—at least for now. The brokers, the manipulators, the corrupt officials—they'd all be exposed. But what would be left when the dust settled? A new exchange? A new way of trading? Or would we just watch as the system crumbled under the weight of its own corruption?

"Let's keep our heads down for now," Stan said, breaking my chain of thought. "There's a long road ahead. We've got to be ready for whatever comes next."

We nodded in agreement, each of us silently preparing for the fallout that was sure to come. The market was in freefall, and the world was watching. But no matter how bad things got, I knew one thing for sure: we had changed history. And that would be our legacy.

We were standing on the edge of history. Now we just had to survive the fall.

CHAPTER TWENTY-ONE

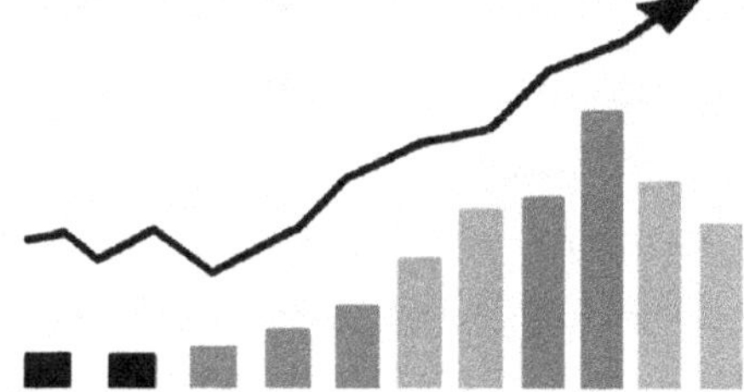

I woke up to the shrill sound of the phone ringing, its insistence cutting through the heavy quiet of the morning. The clock on the nightstand read 5:47 AM, but it might as well have been midnight. After the chaos of Black Monday, I wasn't sure what time even meant anymore.

I reached for the receiver, my hand still shaky from exhaustion. "Yeah?" My voice was hoarse, my throat dry.

"It's Owen." His tone was clipped, all business. "You've seen the news?"

"Not yet," I muttered, sitting up and rubbing my face. "But I can guess. They're calling it the end of the financial world as we know it, right?"

"Pretty much. Turn on Channel 5. It's wall-to-wall coverage."

I grabbed the remote and clicked on the TV. The screen lit up with images of frantic traders, their faces etched with panic, and bold headlines screaming phrases like *'Black Monday Devastates Markets'* and *'Largest Single-Day Loss in U.S. History.'* A ticker at the bottom of the screen scrolled endlessly with falling numbers.

"Jesus," I whispered, running a hand through my hair.

"Yeah," Owen said grimly. "It's bad. But the pit's quieter this morning. The brokers aren't as cocky as they were last week."

"That's not surprising." I stood and walked to the window, pulling back the curtain to let in the pale morning light. The city outside seemed subdued, as if Chicago itself was still in shock.

Owen let out a short laugh, but there was no humor in it. "Funny how it took a market collapse for them to finally shut up."

The memory of yesterday's chaos hit me like a wave—the shouting, the frantic hand signals, the fear in the eyes of even the most seasoned traders. "It's not just the brokers," I said, my voice low. "Everyone's scared, Owen. And they should be."

He paused for a moment before replying. "Scared or not, we've done our part. The S&P pit isn't the same, and we made damn sure of that."

"Yeah, but this crash... it's showing cracks even deeper than we imagined. The ban on dual trading fixed one problem, but the whole system's fragile."

"Fragile is an understatement," Owen said bitterly. "It's like building a house on quicksand."

A knock at the door startled me. "Hang on, someone's here."

"Honey! Stan is here!" Shannon called out from the kitchen.

"It's Stan," I said to Owen.

"Alright. Call me back," he said before hanging up.

I opened the door to find Stan's face drawn. He held up a newspaper, the headline screaming *'Who's to Blame for Black Monday?'*

"Good morning," he said, stepping inside without waiting for an invitation.

"Barely," I replied, gesturing for him to take a seat.

"Good morning, Stan. Coffee?" Shannon's warm voice lifted Stan's spirit a bit.

"Good morning beautiful Shannon! Yes, thank you." Shannon poured a cup and slid it toward Stan, who caught it gracefully.

"Well, I'm off to work. You two behave, okay?"

"Yes, ma'am!" We both said in unison.

Shannon laughed at us, kissed me goodbye, and left. She didn't know but I watched her by our window every morning until she disappeared beyond the horizon. My greatest fear was losing her.

"Mikey," Stan groaned, sinking into the chair like a man carrying the weight of the world.

As I poured another two mugs of coffee, he flipped the paper onto the kitchen counter. "They're already pointing fingers. Brokers, investors, the exchanges. You name it."

I handed him a cup and sat down across from him. "And where do they land on us?"

Stan took a sip and grimaced, probably at both the coffee and the situation. "We're not front-page villains, at least not yet. But you know it's coming. The CME's negligence is going to be in the spotlight, especially with the FBI sniffing around now."

"They're looking for more than negligence," I said, staring at the dark liquid in my mug. "They're digging for rot, and they're going to find it."

Stan rocked on his chair. "And when they do, what's left of the CME?"

I didn't have an answer. Instead, I thought about the S&P pit, the shouts, the chaos, the quick-witted traders who could read a market's pulse like doctors reading a heart monitor. It had always been a wild, unpredictable place, but it had been ours. And now, it was quieter, almost subdued. The brokers weren't swaggering around like kings anymore. The independent traders stood a little taller, their confidence bolstered by the reforms we'd fought so hard to implement.

"We've changed things," I said finally. "That's got to count for something."

Stan nodded slowly. "It does. But Michael, you know as well as I do that this crash is going to bring everything to the surface—everything. And we're right in the middle of it."

"Good," I said, surprising even myself with the conviction in my voice. "Let it all come out. If the system's broken, it needs to break completely before it can be rebuilt."

Stan raised an eyebrow but didn't argue. Instead, he finished his coffee in one long gulp and stood. "You're going to the floor today?"

"Of course," I said, standing too. "Where else would I be?"

As he left, I glanced back at the TV. The images of panic and collapse hadn't changed.

The trading floor was quieter than I expected when I arrived. Not calm, not by any stretch of the imagination, but there was a distinct shift. The usual roaring cacophony of voices was replaced by sharp, clipped conversations and hurried exchanges. Every face I passed looked tense, drawn, and pale.

"Michael!" Owen's voice cut through the hum of tension as he waved me over to our usual corner near the edge of the S&P pit.

As I approached, he leaned in close, his expression grim. "You feel it?"

"Hard to miss," I replied, scanning the room. The brokers looked different today. Their usual cocky swagger was gone, replaced by something I hadn't seen before: vulnerability.

"They're scrambling," Owen said, nodding toward a cluster of brokers huddled near one of the clearing firms. "Without dual trading, they've got no safety net."

I watched as one of the brokers, a tall guy I vaguely recognized, gestured wildly at another, his face red with frustration. Their heated argument ended with the second broker throwing up his hands and walking away, leaving the first looking completely deflated.

"They can't hide behind their split roles anymore," I said, the realization settling in. "Every move they make is out in the open now."

"Exactly," Owen said, his tone carrying a mix of satisfaction and caution. "It's forcing them to actually trade, not exploit."

Stan joined us a moment later, carrying his clipboard like it was a shield. "The reforms are holding," he said without preamble. "Even with this crash, they can't sidestep the rules anymore. No more playing both sides."

I nodded. "And no more skimming profits off trades that never should've happened."

"That's the thing," Stan said, his voice lowering. "It's exposing how weak their game really was. Most of these guys don't know how to operate without their little tricks. They're floundering."

We stood there for a moment, watching the pit. The independent traders, though clearly rattled by the market collapse, seemed to be adapting. They weren't immune to the chaos, but they weren't drowning in it either.

Owen glanced at me, a faint smirk tugging at his lips. "Kind of poetic, isn't it? The guys who swore we were ruining the system are the ones falling apart."

I couldn't help but smile, though it was bittersweet. "Yeah, but we both know this isn't over. The crash might shield the CME for now, but the FBI isn't going anywhere."

Stan frowned. "They're digging deeper. I overheard one of the agents this morning—something about auditing old trade tickets. They're not just looking for dual trading anymore; they're looking for patterns, schemes, anything they can use to build their case."

I let out a slow breath, the weight of his words pressing on my chest. "And they'll find it," I said. "We know how deep this goes. We've seen it."

Owen's smirk faded, replaced by a determined look. "Let them find it. The more they uncover, the harder it'll be for anyone to deny how broken this place was."

Stan gave a curt nod. "The reforms bought us time, but the fight's far from over. This crash is the beginning of something bigger."

As we talked, a broker near the edge of the pit suddenly slammed his hand against the counter, his voice loud enough to carry across the room. "This is a goddamn disaster!"

Heads turned, but no one said anything.

"They're watching us," I said, more to myself than to the others.

"Who?" Owen asked.

"Everyone," I replied. "The brokers, the traders, the media, the FBI. They're all watching to see if this place can hold together."

Stan's gaze followed mine, his expression unreadable. "It will," he said firmly.

The FBI presence on the trading floor wasn't just a shadow anymore—it was a full-blown storm. Over the next few days, agents moved through the CME with purpose, their plain blue jackets standing out starkly against the chaotic swirl of the trading pits. It wasn't hard to see that they were closing in, their quiet inquiries turning into overt interviews and demands for records.

Rumors flew like wildfire, and the brokers who had once lorded over the pits now skulked around like hunted animals. It was clear: the feds weren't here to play games, they were building a case.

Owen dropped a stack of papers onto the desk next to me with a thud. "You hear the latest?" he asked.

"What now?" I asked, barely looking up.

"They're talking indictments," he said, pulling up a chair. "Key players. High-profile names. It's not just about dual trading anymore, Michael. They're linking this to broader fraud—wash trading, front-running, money laundering, you name it."

I exhaled slowly, the weight of his words settling over me. "They've been investigating for months. Years, probably. Dual trading was just the tip of the iceberg."

Owen leaned closer, his voice dropping to a whisper. "You think Vince is in trouble?"

I glanced across the room at Vince, who was standing near the pit, his usual stoic demeanor intact. "If anyone can keep his head above water, it's him," I said. "But let's not pretend he didn't know how the game was played."

Owen gave a grim nod. "Nobody in this place is clean. Not completely."

Just then, Stan appeared. "They've subpoenaed the clearing firms," he said, sitting down heavily. "Every trade, every account, they're pulling it all."

"Good," I said, surprising even myself with the steel in my voice. "Let them see it. Let the whole world see what this place has been hiding."

Stan looked at me, his expression sharp. "You know what this means, right? The CME's reputation is going to take a hit it might not recover from. Traders are already jumping ship. Confidence is in freefall."

"Better the truth comes out now than later," I replied. "We've already done our part. The reforms are holding. Dual trading is gone. That's something."

"But is it enough?" Owen asked, his tone skeptical. "What if this whole place collapses under the weight of its own corruption?"

I didn't have an answer. None of us did.

That afternoon, FBI Agent Richards stood on the platform overlooking the main floor and declared an announcement. His voice carried over the hum of activity as he addressed the room.

"Ladies and gentlemen," the agent began, his voice cutting through the chaos, "as part of our ongoing investigation, federal indictments have been issued against several individuals associated with this exchange. These charges include fraud, conspiracy, and other criminal activities that have undermined the integrity of the market."

The room exploded.

"Fraud?!" one broker shouted, his voice dripping with indignation.

"This is a witch hunt!" another bellowed.

"You've got the wrong people!" someone yelled, his face red with rage.

Others, perhaps more guilty than they dared to admit, tried to blend into the crowd, their darting eyes and pale faces giving them away. Then, the arrests began. Agents moved with precision, pulling individuals aside. A few went quietly, their heads bowed. But others resisted, shouting as they were led away.

"I didn't do anything! This is bullshit!" one man yelled, his voice echoing through the pit.

Another broke free momentarily, only to be subdued again. "You'll hear from my lawyer!" he screamed, his words more desperate than threatening.

I stood frozen, watching as the scene unfolded like something out of a bad dream.

Owen clapped a hand on my shoulder, his grip firm. "We did the right thing, Michael," he said, his voice steady despite the chaos around us. "Whatever happens now, we did what we could to fix this place."

I nodded, though the knot in my stomach didn't loosen. "We pulled out the rotten plank, but the whole ship might go down."

Stan, who had been standing nearby with arms crossed, spoke up. "Then it wasn't a ship worth saving."

Across the floor, Brad stood with his arms crossed, a wry grin tugging at his lips. "Look at 'em scramble," he muttered, loud enough for me to hear. Next to him, Steve stifled a laugh, clearly enjoying the downfall of men who had built their empires on lies. Vince watched, being oddly quiet, and I could see the satisfaction in the eyes of the twenty-five men who fought for the S&P.

For years, the CME had been a playground for greed, where rules were bent or broken to benefit the few at the expense of the many. Now the curtain had been pulled back, and the world could see what really lay beneath the polished surface. By the end of the day, the indictments dominated every conversation. The whispers were no longer speculative—names had been named, though notably not Dave Patterson or any of the brokers in the S&P 500 pit. The men who had ruled the trading floors with arrogance now faced charges that could end their careers, their freedom, or both.

As I left the building that evening, I couldn't shake the feeling of unease. The fight to ban dual trading had been about cleaning up the S&P pit and restoring fairness to a corrupt system. But the FBI's investigation had exposed an even deeper rot—one I hadn't fully grasped before. The FBI's presence loomed over the CME like a dark cloud, and yet, amidst the chaos, I couldn't help but see the irony in it all.

The crash had laid bare the market's fragility, and the federal investigation had exposed corruption that ran deeper than I had imagined. But even as the foundations of the exchange were being shaken, the reforms we had fought for—eliminating dual trading in the S&P pit—remained steadfast.

For all the noise and upheaval, that one change had brought a measure of stability to the chaos. Brokers who had once exploited their dual roles for personal gain now found themselves stripped of that advantage. They had to adapt, forced to operate under rules they could no longer bend.

CHAPTER TWENTY-TWO

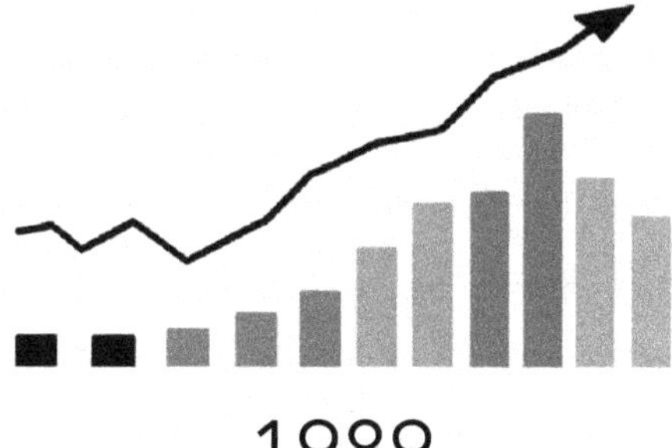

1989

THE CHICAGO TRIBUNE

January 15, 1989

THE FALL OF DUAL TRADING: HOW AN ANONYMOUS GROUP OF REFORMERS HELPED SAVE THE S&P

CHICAGO, IL *- On the chaotic trading floor of the Chicago Mercantile Exchange (CME), where fortunes are made and lost in seconds, a quiet revolution has reshaped the S&P 500 futures pit. This seismic shift comes in the aftermath of an unprecedented investigation by the Federal Bureau of Investigation (FBI), exposing systemic corruption tied to the controversial practice of dual trading. At the center of this transformation is an* *anonymous group of twenty-five traders whose efforts helped usher in reforms that many argue saved the market's integrity.*

The Systemic Problem of Dual Trading

Dual trading, a practice allowing brokers to trade on behalf of their clients while also trading for their personal accounts, was once a cornerstone of the CME's operations. Proponents claimed it enhanced liquidity and ensured the smooth execution of trades. Critics, however, warned it was a breeding ground for conflicts of interest, fraud, and exploitation.

"Brokers had too much power," one former trader explained. "They could front-run client orders, taking advantage of privileged information to profit personally. It was an open secret that the system favored the few at the expense of everyone else."

The warnings turned out to be prescient. By 1987, the FBI had launched a covert investigation into the CME and the Chicago Board of Trade (CBOT), deploying undercover agents and recording hundreds of hours of conversations. The investigation culminated in several high-profile indictments, revealing a culture of corruption deeply entrenched in Chicago's futures markets.

The Role of the FBI

The FBI's operation, nicknamed "Project Sour Mash," focused on fraudulent activities enabled by dual trading. Agents discovered brokers manipulating trades, falsifying records, and engaging in collusion to maximize their profits at the expense of clients and the broader market. In 1988, federal prosecutors announced indictments against multiple individuals, charging them with fraud, conspiracy, and other crimes.

One FBI agent, speaking on condition of anonymity, described the atmosphere on the trading floor during the investigation: "It was chaos. The traders were loud and brash, but beneath the noise was a very calculated system of exploitation. Dual trading wasn't just a loophole; it was a business model."

The Anonymous Reformers

Amid this turmoil, a group of twenty-five independent traders emerged as unlikely heroes. Operating in secrecy to avoid retaliation, these reformers campaigned tirelessly to ban dual trading in the S&P 500 futures pit. Their motivations were not purely altruistic; they had seen firsthand how the practice undermined the market's integrity and eroded trust among traders.

"We knew it was a risk," one member of the group said in an anonymous interview. "But we also knew the system couldn't continue the way it was. If we didn't act, the corruption would only get worse."

The group faced intense opposition. Brokers, fearing the loss of lucrative opportunities, launched smear campaigns, whispered threats, and even engaged in physical intimidation. Yet the reformers persevered, eventually gaining enough support to push for changes that banned dual trading in the S&P pit by 1987.

Black Monday: A Catalyst for Change

The stock market crash of October 19, 1987, known as Black Monday, underscored the urgent need for reform. The largest single-day percentage drop in U.S. market history exposed vulnerabilities in the financial system, with dual trading receiving fresh scrutiny. While the crash devastated institutions and traders alike, the newly implemented ban on dual trading in the S&P pit provided a measure of stability.

"If dual trading hadn't been eliminated," a market analyst noted, "the fallout from Black Monday could have been even worse. The reforms forced brokers to play by stricter rules, preventing further abuses during an already volatile period."

The Aftermath

The FBI's investigation and the resulting indictments have sent shockwaves through the CME. Several brokers have been convicted, with sentences ranging from hefty fines to prison terms. The exchange itself has been forced to implement sweeping reforms to restore its tarnished reputation.

Despite the upheaval, the efforts of the anonymous twenty-five are widely regarded as a turning point. Their campaign to eliminate dual trading has been credited with laying the groundwork for a fairer, more transparent market.

"They took an incredible risk," said a CME official who declined to be named. "Without their push for change, the exchange might not have survived this crisis."

A Market Transformed

Today, the S&P 500 futures pit operates under a new set of rules, reflecting the hard-won reforms of the past few years. The culture of impunity that once defined the CME has been replaced by a cautious optimism as traders adapt to a landscape where integrity is no longer optional.

For the reformers, the fight was about more than just the mechanics of trading.

"We weren't just fighting for ourselves," one member of the group said. "We were fighting for everyone who believes in fair markets. It was messy, it was painful, but it was worth it."

As the FBI's work continues, the lessons of Chicago's trading floors resonate far beyond the Windy City. The fall of dual trading serves as a reminder that even in the most cutthroat environments, reform is possible—if enough people are willing to stand up and demand it.

I folded the newspaper, its edges crisp and crackling. The scent of freshly brewed coffee hung in the air, its warmth wrapped around me like an old friend. I set the paper down with a deliberate motion, the bold headline glaring up at me, unwavering and unforgiving. The words seemed to pulse on the page, each letter a reminder of something I had tried to bury. My heart thudded in my chest, not with the heavy beat of fear, but with the quiet, insistent rhythm of relief.

"Shannon," I called out, my voice steady despite the turmoil inside me. "You need to read this."

She appeared in the doorway a moment later, dish towel in hand. Her movements were slow and graceful, and her red hair glowed in the early morning light. She locked her eyes on mine and the furrow on her brow deepened.

"What is it?" she asked, her voice laced with concern.

I didn't say anything more; instead, I slid the newspaper across the counter toward her, the edges curling slightly.

"Just... read," I urged softly.

She picked it up, her fingers trembling ever so slightly as she unfolded it. Her eyes danced across the words at first, scanning, trying to make sense of what she was reading. I watched her face closely, noting the subtle changes as her expression shifted from curiosity to something more intense. A flicker of recognition, of something unspoken, passed through her eyes. As she continued reading, her face tightened, her lips quivered, and her shoulders tensed as if bracing against an unseen storm. When her gaze reached the part about the anonymous group of twenty-five men, she froze, her hand instinctively coming up to cover her mouth.

"Oh, Michael..." she whispered, her voice thick with emotion, as though the weight of the words had finally reached her heart. Her eyes welled up with tears, the fight to keep them at bay clear in the quick blink that followed. "They told your story. They finally told it."

I nodded, swallowing hard, feeling a lump form in my throat as well. The flood of emotions, relief, anger, regret, but above all, a quiet sense of vindication, was almost overwhelming.

"Yeah. They did."

She placed the paper down on the counter gently, her touch almost reverent, as if the printed words held more power than just ink on paper. She took a step closer to me, her eyes searching mine, and her voice softened.

"It's about damn time. After everything you've been through—after everything we've been through..." Her voice faltered again, unable to finish the sentence. She wrapped her arms around me, pulling me into a tight embrace. "I'm so proud of you."

In that moment, the world outside seemed to fall away. It wasn't just the weight of the past few years that pressed down on me, but the sheer magnitude of what we had endured together. It wasn't a victory over the outside forces that had tried to tear us apart, but a quiet acknowledgment of the strength that had kept us intact. I held her close, feeling the weight of all the unanswered questions and the lingering ache of old wounds begin to lift, even if just for a moment.

"It's not just me," I whispered, my voice thick with the emotion I had been hiding for so long. "It was all of us. We couldn't have done it alone."

She pulled back slightly, her hands still resting gently on my arms. She studied me with a tenderness that seemed to pierce through the layers of my armor.

"But you were part of it. And that matters."

I leaned down and kissed her forehead, a small gesture that spoke volumes. "Thanks, Shan."

After a beat, I stepped back, my jacket slipping easily over my shoulders as I straightened up. The weight of the day ahead loomed, but it was different now, less oppressive.

"Time to get to work," I said.

THE HUM OF THE TRADING FLOOR GREETED ME AS I STEPPED INTO the pit. It was like walking into a storm after breakfast with Shannon. For years, this place had been a battlefield but today, it felt different.

"Morning, Brad," I called, slapping him hard on the back as I passed. He nearly stumbled forward but caught himself with a laugh.

"What the fuck are you eating, boy?" He feigned a back injury. "Morning, kid. Hell of an article, huh?" he said with a grin.

"Hell of a thing," I agreed, catching the gleam of satisfaction in his eyes. "Makes us sound like legends, doesn't it?"

Brad chuckled. "You're telling me. Can't wait to tell my mother about it. She thinks I'm still working at that pizza place in college. Imagine that?"

I snorted. "That actually makes sense..."

"What the fuck—"

"Anyway, bye Brad!" I scurried off into the crowd with a smirk. Pissing off Brad was a new hobby of mine, ever since the FBI cleaned up this place.

Further into the pit, I saw Vince standing in his usual confident posture, though today his smile had a hidden message.

"Good morning, Vince," I greeted him.

"Morning, Michael," he replied with a tone almost lighter than usual. "Let's see if today's as good as the paper says it'll be."

"Yeah, if the article's right, we'll all be on yachts by Friday," I said, raising an eyebrow.

Vince snorted. "I'd settle for a decent lunch at this point."

A few steps later, I spotted Dave Patterson leaning against the edge of the pit.

"Dave," I said, my tone neutral.

He glanced at me, his expression unreadable. "Michael."

I didn't linger. There wasn't much to say between us anymore. But I caught a flicker of regret in his eyes. Owen and Steve were already in the thick of it, their hands flying as they made trades.

"Owen! Steve!" I called out beaming at them.

"Michael!" Steve yelled back, his voice full of energy. "Let's make some money!"

"Easy, Steve, we've got all day," Owen said, not missing a beat. He shot me a quick grin. "Good to see you, man. Let's crush it today."

I stepped into my spot, feeling the familiar rhythm of the floor settle over me. The first trade came quickly, a straightforward order with no complications. Then another. And another. Each one clean, each one solid. The articles, the headlines, they weren't just ink on paper anymore. They were motivation. By midday, my ledger was looking good and the pit was buzzing with a nervous energy that felt more like hope than panic.

Owen leaned over, a rare grin on his face. "Not a bad day, huh?"

"Not bad at all," I replied, a sense of satisfaction settling over me. "This is what we've been waiting for, right?"

"You kidding?" Owen laughed. "If we had any more luck, we'd be buying beachfront property in Malibu by the end of the week."

I looked around, taking it all in. The brokers, the traders, the noise, the chaos, it was still the CME, but it was also something new. Something better. The rules had changed, the players had shifted, and the game was no longer rigged against us.

The buzz around the pit grew, and I could hear Brad in the background hollering, "Who's buying the first round tonight, huh? I'm putting my money on Vince! He owes me!"

Vince shot him a look. "I'll pay for drinks when I hit a million, Brad. Until then, you're on your own."

I couldn't help but laugh.

CHAPTER TWENTY-THREE

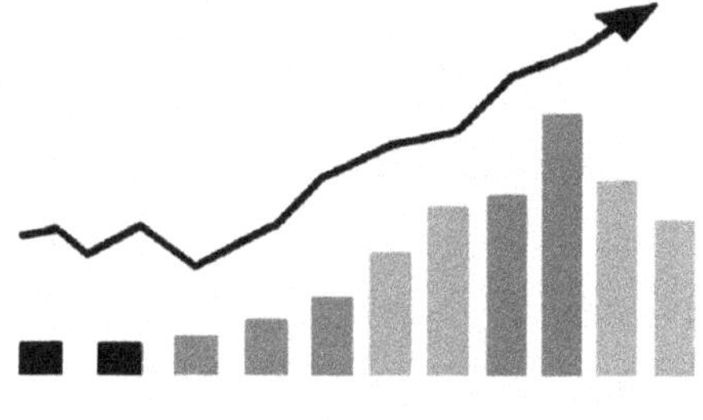

March 1989

Stepping onto the trading floor was like plunging into the heart of a storm. The noise hit me first. Bodies moved in a blur, trading hand signals like a second language. It was chaos, pure and simple. But today, it was like the floor was holding its breath as it waited for the other shoe to drop, even though we all knew it wouldn't. I navigated my way through the pit, dodging bodies and sidestepping shouting traders, but I couldn't shake the feeling that something had shifted. The energy was still fast-paced and unpredictable, but it was more contained now.

"Morning, Brad," I called out as I passed him. He was hunched over his screen, hands flying over the keyboard. His face lit up the moment he saw me.

"Morning, Michael," he replied, his eyes practically sparkling. There was an energy about him today that matched the buzz of the floor.

Forty-six indictments. The scandal had shaken the CME to its foundations. Corruption, deceit, broken trust, it had all been laid bare for the world to see. But somehow, our pit had remained untouched. The S&P futures pit. The one we'd worked tirelessly to protect and fought tooth and nail to implement reforms that no one believed would stick. But somehow, against all odds, they had.

Brad chuckled, "It's kind of wild, right? Who would've thought those reforms actually worked?"

I snorted, unable to keep the smile from creeping onto my face. "Yeah, I was half-expecting us to get dragged down with the rest of them."

Brad's grin only widened. "Not a chance. We fought too damn hard. Couldn't be taken down that easy."

I nodded, though it hadn't been easy. It still wasn't. But today, for the first time in a long while, it felt like we were in control of the chaos. As I moved down the floor, I glanced at the familiar faces of traders and brokers. Vince stood near the railing, his usual stoic self, but today he had a subtle grin playing on his lips. His calm presence always anchored the floor, even when the chaos seemed to take over.

"Vince," I called out, walking over to him.

"Michael," he replied with a nod, his voice even, but there was something different in the way he said it. "Not bad, huh?"

"Yeah, not bad at all," I said, my tone lighter than usual. There was a calm in the air that I hadn't felt in years. The floor was still buzzing, but it wasn't frantic. It was... steady. "Let's just hope it holds," I added, scanning the traders around us. Their voices whispered in quick, anxious bursts as they discussed the fallout from the indictments, speculating about who would be next. There was a palpable sense of disbelief in the air, mixed with relief. It was as if the weight of the past few years was finally being lifted, and we were all starting to realize that we might actually have a future here after all.

As I made my way deeper into the pit, I couldn't help but think about how much we'd all sacrificed. Even Dave, the man who'd tried to take me out, was walking free today, probably unaware of just how close he'd come to a much worse fate.

"Michael!" Steve's voice rang out from across the pit, "Let's make some money today!"

I laughed and gave him a nod. "That's the plan, Steve."

The pit felt different. The usual chaos was still there, but there was an undercurrent of satisfaction that hadn't been present before. The same faces I'd passed countless times, the ones that had looked at me with disdain or suspicion for so long, now gave me brief nods or offered tentative smiles. The FBI's crackdown on corruption had changed things, and now even those who had once looked down on us for pushing for reforms were starting to see us in a different light.

It was an ironic twist. For years, we had been the outcasts—the renegades, the troublemakers who wanted to shake up the system and challenge the status quo. We had been ostracized, threatened, and told that our efforts would fail. But now, as the dust settled from the FBI's sweeping investigation, it was clear that we had been right all along. The reforms we fought for, the ones that had nearly cost us everything, had ultimately saved the brokers in the S&P futures pit. The same pit that had been untouched while others were swept up in the aftermath.

I moved through the floor, a quiet satisfaction settling in my chest. The energy was still frantic, but the tension had shifted. The traders who had once viewed us as the enemy were now nodding, giving us a newfound respect. But just as the wave of relief and satisfaction was settling over me, I felt a tap on my shoulder. I turned, and there he was—Dave Patterson.

"Michael," he said as his eyes avoided mine for a brief moment before meeting my gaze.

I said nothing at first and just sized him up. He'd once been my adversary, and despite everything, I couldn't shake the tension that still lingered between us. He was free now, his name not among the list of those facing charges. Thanks to the very reforms we had pushed for. I knew that, and he knew it, too.

"You're looking... free," I said, my voice edged with anger.

Dave shifted uncomfortably. His eyes flickered around the pit and his hands wrung nervously. It wasn't like him to look unsure, but there was something in his demeanor that told me he wasn't feeling as confident as he usually did.

"Yeah, well... I owe you that, don't I?" he said, finally meeting my gaze with a mixture of guilt and resignation. "The reforms... they saved me. And I'm sure I'm not the only one who's grateful for that."

I narrowed my eyes. "Grateful? Funny, I don't remember you being so grateful when you were trying to take me out."

His expression faltered, and he cleared his throat.

"I've got a lot of things I need to make right, Michael," he said quietly. "And... I need to apologize for what happened. What I did."

I raised an eyebrow. This wasn't the Dave Patterson I knew. The one who'd never backed down, never apologized, never admitted weakness. This was new. And it felt strange.

"I know you're probably not interested in hearing it," he continued, looking regretful.

He looked down for a moment, visibly crumbling under the weight of his own admission. "I... I don't expect forgiveness, Michael. I know that doesn't come easy. But I need you to know, I was the one who sent that guy to shoot you. It was me. I wanted you out of the way."

The confession hit like a punch to the gut. My mind raced back to that night, to the moment everything had changed. The hitman, the gunshot, the months of wondering who wanted me dead, and now here he was, standing before me, admitting it was him. I felt the blood rush to my face, my fists clenching so hard my knuckles cracked. Every instinct I had screamed at me to make him pay.

This guy tried to end my life? The same man who was standing in front of me now, apologizing, admitting guilt? It was surreal.

Without thinking, I took a step toward him, my body trembling with a rush of anger I hadn't felt in years. My breath came quicker, my vision narrowing. I could feel the heat of the rage building, everything in me wanting to lash out, to make him feel the same fear I'd felt when I thought my life was over.

"Michael," Dave said, his voice faltering as he took a half-step back, his eyes wide, almost pleading. "I... I was wrong. I... I never meant for it to go that far. Please, you have to believe me."

But I didn't want to hear it. I didn't care about his regret. I wanted him to feel the same terror, the same anger, the same pain that had haunted me for months. I could already see it in my mind. Just as I raised my arm, a hand clamped down on my shoulder, firm and steady.

"Owen," I spat, my eyes wild. "Get off me."

But Owen didn't budge. His grip only tightened, his voice low but commanding. "Michael, don't. Don't make this about that. You've fought for too much. Don't let this one guy drag you back into it."

I shook my head, barely able to hear his words over the blood rushing in my ears. I felt like I was on the edge of something irreversible, and I didn't know if I wanted to step back from it. My whole body was screaming for retaliation. But Owen, as always, knew me too well.

"Listen to me," Owen said, his voice quieter now, but no less urgent. "You've already won, Michael. This moment? It's not worth it. You know that. Think about what we've done. Think about everything we've fought for."

I breathed heavily, trying to steady myself, feeling the tension in my arm where Owen's hand held me in place. I wanted to strike. I wanted to slam Dave's face into the floor for everything he'd done. But slowly, the fog of anger lifted just enough for me to see reason. Just enough to realize that getting lost in this would mean losing everything we had built. I let out a slow breath, stepping back, my fist unclenching.

"You're lucky," I muttered, my voice still thick with anger but laced with self-control. "You're lucky Owen stepped in. Because I would've killed you, Patterson. Like you wanted to kill me. You'll have to live with that for the rest of your life."

Dave looked down, his eyes still full of guilt and shame. He didn't try to speak anymore, just stood there dumbstruck in the wake of his confession, waiting for whatever came next.

I looked at Owen. "Let's get back to work," I said, the words feeling like an anchor to pull me back to reality. My legs felt heavy as I turned away from Dave, forcing myself to focus on the chaos of the pit once more.

Owen clapped me on the back. "That was close," he said, his voice a mix of relief and humor.

I exhaled and tried to push the rest of the anger out of my system. "Yeah. Too close."

The pit was alive around us, but it wasn't just the regular rhythm of trading. There was a subtle but undeniable change. I took a few steps forward, trying to shake the memory of Dave's words from my mind. There was still a weight on my chest from the anger, but it wasn't the same as before. It felt lighter, as if something inside me had finally cracked open and released the pressure that had built up over the years. Owen fell into step beside me, his pace matching mine.

"You good?" he asked.

"Yeah," I replied, the word feeling strange in my mouth. "I'm good."

We walked past the rows of traders, many of them still buzzing with the aftermath of the FBI's investigation. Some were animated, others quieter than usual, whispers about the indictments echoing through the pit. The power dynamics had shifted. The ones who had once looked down on us, who had dismissed our reforms and threatened us for daring to challenge the system, were suddenly unsure of their place in this new world.

The truth was, we were outsiders. We'd always been the renegades, the ones pushing for change when no one else would. We'd been dismissed, threatened, ostracized. But now, they were looking at us differently. A few brokers shot me knowing glances in passing. The tension of the past had melted into something almost respectful. The reforms had saved the brokers who might have been dragged into the scandal. They had kept us out of the wreckage. And for all the years of fight, the ones who had once been the outcasts were now the ones who had changed the game. I slid into my position, my hands still shaking slightly.

Owen gave me a quick glance as he took his own spot. "You good to go?"

I nodded, a small smile breaking through the tension. "Yeah. Let's get to work."

He was already sliding into his rhythm, his focus sharp as he scanned the numbers on his screen.

We might have been dismissed once, but now we stood as the unsung heroes of this place. The ones who had faced the corruption head-on and lived to see it crumble. And as I took a breath, the noise of the floor buzzing in my ears, I couldn't help but feel like, finally, it was all worth it. Everything we had done, every sacrifice, every risk, had been for this moment. And now, the S&P futures pit was ours.

As the day wore on and the trades continued, my mind lingered on the road we had traveled. It was a long, hard road filled with moments of doubt, fear, and betrayal, but it was also a road that led us to victory. To a legacy we would carry with us for the rest of our lives. Owen's voice cut through my thoughts.

"You think this is the end of it?"

I shook my head as my eyes scanned the floor.

"No. But it's a damn good start."

And as I glanced around at the faces of my allies, I knew one thing for sure: we had changed the fucking game.

EPILOGUE

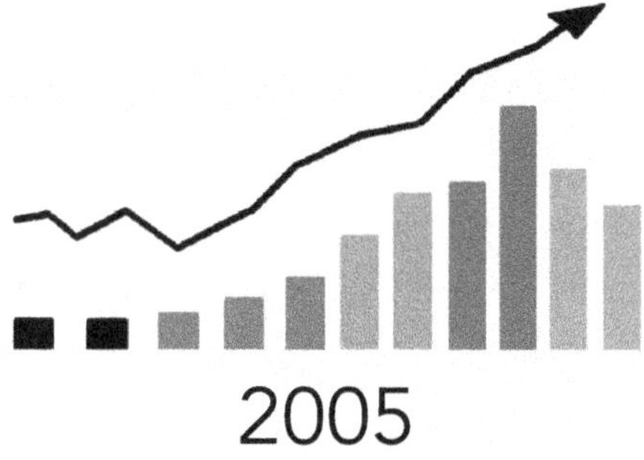

2005

Years had passed since the chaos of the trading floor, the FBI's investigations, the reforms, and the battle for justice that had torn through the heart of the Chicago Mercantile Exchange (CME). The noise, the intensity, the high stakes, everything about that world had faded in my rearview mirror, but not without leaving its mark. Time had softened the edges of those memories, but there were still moments when I could hear the shouting, feel the rush of adrenaline, and remember the taste of victory, bitter as it had been.

I stood at the window of my office, looking out over the bustling city. The skyline was familiar, but the view was different now. The chaos that had once thrived in the pits of the CME was now tempered with something more controlled. The reforms we had fought for, those years of struggle, had transformed the exchange. I could still hear the ghosts of the old days, the whispers of corruption, the pressure of the system designed to protect the powerful. But now, the future seemed clearer, more transparent.

It wasn't perfect, but it was better. And that was something.

In 2005, things had begun to change for the CME. The transformation was slow but steady. The CME had begun shifting from its traditional open outcry system to a more automated and electronic platform for trading, with the launch of the CME Globex trading system in the late 1990s and its expansion in the early 2000s. This was the same platform that had been crucial in handling the new wave of regulation and reform that followed the corporate scandals of the late 1990s. The push for transparency and fairness had finally started to take root. The exchanges were moving toward a more regulated, secure environment where market manipulation and insider trading were less likely to thrive.

"Hey, you're not planning on retiring early, are you?" Shannon's voice broke my reverie.

I turned, smiling at her as she entered the room, her presence always grounding me. Shannon had been there through it all, through the betrayals, the fights, the long nights when I couldn't sleep because I was haunted by what we'd been up against. I could see the changes in her, too. How motherhood had softened her, made her more patient, yet also more fierce in her own way.

"No, just thinking," I said, my voice betraying the depth of my thoughts.

She raised an eyebrow, her smile playful yet knowing. "About how many years you've been telling me the same thing?"

I laughed, stepping toward her. "Yeah, I guess that's been my thing, huh?"

We shared a quiet moment, the kind we hadn't had in a long while. There was peace in the air now, a peace that felt earned but fragile. And in that moment, I knew it wasn't just the city or the exchange that had changed, it was me. The man I'd been years ago, driven by anger, vengeance, and a need for retribution, was no longer the man standing in front of her. I'd found something else, something real, something worth holding onto when I looked into Shannon's eyes.

"Come on, let's take a walk," she said, breaking the silence again. "You can keep thinking while we stretch our legs."

I reluctantly agreed and we left the office, making our way down to the street. Outside, the world was bustling as always, but it felt different now. It was a different city, one that had evolved with time, just like the CME had. And I had changed with it.

I hadn't been back to the exchange in months, not since I'd officially stepped away from the day-to-day. The noise of the trading floor had been replaced by the quieter hum of management, policy changes, and regulatory oversight. The reform we'd fought for had done more than clean up the mess. It had set a new standard. Transparency. Accountability. Fairness. It was everything the old guard had fought against, and everything we had fought for.

As we made our way back through the familiar streets, I couldn't help but think of those days. The days when the CME had been a battlefield. I remembered the night we'd gotten word of the indictments, how the ground had felt like it was shifting beneath us. The brokers who had fought with us had all played their part in changing the game. And while we'd never been the ones to make headlines, we had shifted the tide—one battle at a time.

"Do you remember that night?" I asked Shannon, my eyes lingering on the CME building in the distance. "When the indictments came down? It felt like the world was cracking open."

Shannon glanced at me, her expression thoughtful. "I remember. It was like the calm before the storm, and then, boom, everything changed. I still remember the look on your face when the news hit. Like you knew things were never going to be the same."

"I did know," I said, the weight of those memories coming back. "The floor was never going to be the same after that. The way we had to fight to make the changes, it was all worth it, but it came at such a cost."

She nodded quietly, squeezing my hand as we walked. "But you did it. You didn't back down. And that's why things are different now. You were part of that change, Michael."

I smiled, looking down at her. "I don't know about that. But I know we gave the CME a chance. And that's enough for me."

The world saw the FBI's investigation as the end of something. The beginning of accountability. The collapse of the corrupt structure that had governed the markets for decades. But for us, the renegades, the ones who had pushed for reform when no one else would, it was just the start of something new. A new order. And while the credit was given to the authorities who swooped in and cleaned up the mess, we knew the truth. That we were the ones who had turned the tide. We had been the ones to risk everything for a better future. For the next generation of traders.

"You know," Shannon said after a pause, "I've been thinking about how the whole thing ended. Everyone always talks about the FBI and how they cracked everything wide open, but I think we both know the real heroes. The ones who fought from the inside."

"Yeah," I agreed, a hint of a smile tugging at my lips. "We may not have made the headlines, but we were the ones pushing for change before it was cool."

Shannon let out a small laugh. "You've always been a little stubborn."

I chuckled, shaking my head. "Not stubborn. Just determined."

As we walked, the conversation turned to other things, such as Eliza's—our daughter—upcoming birthday, the neighborhood, and how everything seemed to be changing around us. The small talk felt comforting. But even as we spoke, my mind drifted back to the past. To Dave Patterson.

I hadn't heard from Dave in a while. He had been released after the investigation, no longer the threat he once was. In a strange twist, he had come to me and apologized. It was a quiet thing, no grand gestures, just a man seeking redemption in the aftermath of his mistakes. The confession still lingered in my mind and I could still feel the weight of that moment, the one that had changed everything. But I had let it go. The anger that had driven me for so long had dulled over time, replaced by something more distant. Peace. Forgiveness even, in a way.

"I heard from Dave Patterson the other day," I said, quietly.

Shannon looked at me, surprised. "Really? After all this time?"

"Yeah," I said, nodding. "He apologized, again. No grand speeches or anything, but it was enough to gain my forgiveness."

Shannon stopped walking as she turned to face me. "What did you say to him?"

I hesitated, trying to find the right words. "I told him it was over. That I'd forgiven him. It wasn't easy, but I realized I had to let it go. Holding on to that anger… it wasn't worth it anymore. And I think he needed to hear that."

Shannon looked at me for a long moment before nodding slowly. "I can't say I'm surprised. You've always had a way of seeing the bigger picture, even when it's hard to let go."

I shrugged, feeling the weight of it all. "I'm not sure I always do, but in this case… I think it was the right choice."

She placed her hand on my face and the gentle touch was comforting.

And then there was Shannon.

There was a time when I couldn't imagine life without the constant hum of the floor, without the chaos that had defined my every move. But now, as I stood by her side, watching our daughter grow up together, I couldn't imagine a world without her. Eliza was growing up in a world that had changed because of the fight we'd all put in. She wouldn't know the old CME. She wouldn't have to grow up in the shadow of corruption. She would know a world where fairness wasn't just a dream, it was the foundation.

The next time we were on a walk as a family, I watched Eliza running ahead of us, laughing as she chased a dog that had wandered into the park.

"I hope she doesn't live through the stuff we did," I whispered.

"No," Shannon agreed, her smile full of pride. "She won't. And that's because she has a father who won't allow it."

I watched Eliza for a moment, my heart full of love. "And a mother who would fight any case for her."

Shannon blushed as we continued to walk in silence for a while, the weight of the past lifting slightly with every step. Everything we had fought for had led to this moment of peace and new beginnings.

"You know," Shannon said as we sat on a park bench, "I think Eliza's gonna be pretty proud of you one day."

I looked over at her, catching the glint of pride in her eyes. "You really think so?"

She nodded. "I do. You've built something that matters. More than just money or power. You changed things, and she will know about it."

I felt a lump in my throat. "It didn't always feel like it was going to be worth it. Sometimes, I didn't even know what I was fighting for anymore. I just knew I had to keep going. I couldn't stop."

Shannon smiled softly, squeezing my hand. "And you didn't."

I watched Eliza run around, her laughter carrying in the wind. The future. It was right in front of me, in her innocent smile, in the way she saw the world. And I knew, deep down, that this was the victory. The one that mattered most.

The CME was a different place now, its old ways cleaned up; the corrupt practices replaced with policies that ensured transparency. The exchanges no longer ran on favoritism and backdoor deals; instead, they ran on fairness. The traders now entered the floor with the knowledge that the rules applied to everyone, regardless of who they were. It wasn't perfect, but it was better. And I had been part of that change.

I hadn't expected a medal or recognition for it. The fight had never been about that. But when I looked around the exchange these days, as I watched new traders entering the floor, I knew the truth. We had done it. We had changed the game. We had set the stage for a better future.

Shannon spoke as if reading my mind "You don't need a medal. You know that, right?"

I turned to her, a little surprised by her words. "I guess I thought there'd be some sort of acknowledgment at some point. Something to say that all of this was worth it."

Shannon smiled softly. "You don't need anyone else to tell you that. You already know."

I exhaled slowly, watching my daughter. The world was still noisy, still chaotic. But now, it felt like it had a purpose.

"You're right," I said, my voice more certain than it had been in a long time. "I guess the real victory is that we made it. We changed things, and that matters more than any recognition."

"Look at her," Shannon said softly, watching Eliza chase after a butterfly. "She's so full of life. She doesn't have to worry about the things we did. She's growing up in a world where fairness actually means something."

My eyes traced Eliza's movements and my heart swelled with a bittersweet pride. The future was brighter for her, and that was the most important thing.

Brad. Owen. Vince. Steve. We were the renegades. The outsiders who had been ostracized for wanting something better. Together, we had pushed for the reforms that now defined the exchange.

I thought about Vince, who had always been the strategist in our group. The quiet one, always observing, but when it mattered, he had never hesitated to speak up, to act. He had been the one to put together the game plan for our coalition, the one who believed in transparency even when it seemed like the most impossible dream. His vision had kept us grounded, his calm and reason keeping us focused during the storm.

Brad had been our backbone, the one who would fight in the trenches with us, even when the odds seemed stacked against us. His loyalty had never wavered, and though his sharp tongue had sometimes gotten him into trouble, it had also been his weapon in the battle for change. He was the kind of guy who would take a bullet for you—and who had, metaphorically, many times over.

Owen, always the pragmatic one, had shown up in his own way. His way of seeing the floor, seeing the patterns before anyone else, had helped us understand not just the technicalities, but the human side of things. He had been the one who believed in us when we doubted ourselves. He'd been the one who stayed with me through the roughest times, even when the walls were closing in. The unsung hero of the group, but in his own right, the one who had always known when to act.

And then there was Steve. He had been one of the toughest sons of bitches I'd ever met. He was a man who wore his heart on his sleeve, who had the kind of loyalty you couldn't find anywhere else. A fucking drunkard. But the years of stress, the toll of the fight, had eventually caught up with him. His liver failure came too suddenly, too harshly. We'd lost him, and that loss had hit me harder than I could've ever predicted.

Shannon squeezed my hand and I looked at her lovingly. Trying to imagine a world without her was impossible, and in that moment, I knew the future was going to be great.

As I gazed out at the skyline, a sense of quiet resolve settled over me. The legacy of the renegades would endure, etched into the foundation of the new CME—one built on transparency, fairness, and a system that no longer sheltered corruption. The battles we'd fought, the sacrifices we'd made, had set a new course. It wasn't just about us anymore; it was about the future we'd secured for everyone who came after. We'd paid a heavy price, but it had been worth it. We'd traded everything we had for a better tomorrow. And in the end, it was a damn good trade.

www.ingramcontent.com/pod-product-compliance
Lightning Source LLC
LaVergne TN
LVHW010655110826
845149LV00014B/3107

* 9 7 9 8 9 9 2 6 0 7 6 0 4 *